CW01513339

# Bound to be

# **Boundless**

### The Journey of a Third Culture Kid

BLESSING ADOGAME

Copyright © 2023 Blessing Adogame

All rights reserved.

ISBN: 9798397452120

# DEDICATION

Dedicated with heartfelt gratitude to my extraordinary family: Afe and Esther, my loving parents, and my wonderful siblings, Faith and Midafe. Your unwavering support has been the foundation of my journey, shaping me into the person I am today. This dedication extends to embrace the vibrant community of third-culture kids who, like me, have navigated the unique challenges of straddling multiple cultures. To those who have felt the disorienting sense of being adrift, uncertain of where you truly belong, I offer this book as a companion on your journey. May the stories within these pages resonate with your own experiences and serve as a source of solace, understanding, and inspiration.

# CONTENTS

## THE COMMONALITY OF THE HUMAN EXPERIENCE IS:

Emotions

Relationships

Birth and Death

Growth and Development

Struggles and Challenges

Cultural Expression

Learning and Knowledge

Values and Morality

Search for Meaning

Adaptation and Resilience

While the specifics of these common aspects of the human experience may vary from person to person and culture to culture, they form a foundation that unites all of humanity. Recognizing these commonalities can foster empathy and understanding among people from diverse backgrounds and help bridge cultural and social divides.

So, let's begin…

…with an activity (grab a pen!)

## BOUND OR BOUNDLESS Activity

Before reading ahead, I want to challenge you to reflect on your own sense of limitation and boundlessness through these questions:

**You have an appointment at 5pm and you set your travel schedule to arrive by:**
- A) 4:45pm
- B) 5pm

**Your friend opens up to you about something you did that hurt them. What is your first instinct?**
- A) Apologize
- B) Give an explanation in defense

**How do you answer the "Where are you from?" question.**
- A) The country that I was born
- B) The country that I currently live in (if different)

**When do you go to the doctor?**
- A) Regularly, regardless of if I have a reason
- B) Rarely, only when I need to

**Think about a recent setback. How did it affect your faith and hope?**
- A) It was an opportunity to strengthen my faith and find hope in a new direction.
- B) Felt disheartened and struggled to maintain hope in the face of adversity.

## Let's review!

### If your answers included 3 or more B's, read this...

If you find yourself leaning more towards the "bound" choices in this activity, it's an opportunity to explore the significance of structure and tradition in your life. Your inclination towards the familiar and secure may provide stability, but it's essential to remember that "Bound to be Boundless" holds the promise of pushing you beyond your comfort zone. This book will encourage you to consider how even within boundaries, there can be moments of growth and transformation. Embrace the journey ahead as a chance to find new perspectives within the known, uncovering hidden facets of your world.

---

### If your answers included 3 or more A's, read this...

Your preference for the "boundless" choices suggests a spirit of adventure, innovation, and a willingness to break free from constraints. "Bound to be Boundless" is poised to be a captivating experience that aligns with your disposition. It will inspire you to embrace change, challenge the status quo, and explore the limitless horizons of human potential. As you dive into the pages of the book, be ready to reaffirm and celebrate your boundless nature, while also finding insight into the beauty of structure and tradition that can coexist harmoniously with your adventurous spirit.

## About this Activity

The "Bound or Boundless" activity is designed as a thought-provoking guide, intended to stimulate self-reflection, and encourage readers to explore their own inclinations. It's important to remember that life is rarely black and white, and there are countless shades of gray in between. Cultural, societal, and individual contexts can significantly influence one's responses to these questions.

I acknowledge that each question is subject to interpretation, and the answers can vary widely based on personal experiences, cultural backgrounds, and individual circumstances. Individual responses to these situations may vary depending on cultural norms, reflecting differences in values such as punctuality, empathy, sense of place, and proactive health habits.

"Bound to be Boundless" does not aim to impose a singular perspective but rather to explore the interplay between boundaries and boundlessness, recognizing the intricacies of human experience. The book serves as a canvas upon which you, as a reader, can paint your own interpretations and find resonance with your own unique stories. So, as you delve into the pages of this book, embrace the diversity of human perspectives, and allow my insights to complement your own worldview.

Let's actually begin now.

# INTRODUCTION

I felt like I was standing in the middle of a storm, not knowing whether to walk or to stand still. Standing in the eye (center) of a storm is interesting because the eye is the relatively calm and clear area of the storm. It is the surrounding wall of clouds that is deadly. The wall of clouds was a paralyzing fear. A fear that could sweep me away into its deadly winds if I wasn't careful.

In early 2020, life threw me a curveball — a tumor diagnosis. The news hit hard, leaving me feeling lost and alone. To add a bizarre twist, the official diagnosis came through the cold detachment of an email, stripping away any chance for a compassionate, human touch.

Picture this: I was at the airport, all set to visit a friend in Pittsburgh. In the midst of the hustle and bustle, I opened that email, and reality hit me. The contrast between the vibrant chaos around me and the heavy silence within was surreal. As the weight of the diagnosis sunk in, a weird numbness washed over me, a tangible reaction to the emotional whirlwind sparked by the words on my phone screen. In the midst of this emotional storm, I found myself caught in a paradox: even in the moment when I seemed to feel nothing, the weight of it all pressed down on me in its entirety. The battle I faced was an isolating one, and little did I know that it was about to become even lonelier. Shortly after, the global pandemic, COVID-19, struck, casting an additional layer of solitude over what would be an already challenging journey.

Even when I felt nothing, I felt it completely. It was a lonely battle that was only going to get even more lonely, because shortly after the global pandemic, COVID-19, hit. This pandemic was a storm that the world was not ready for. Shortly before it hit, I paced back and forth thinking about whether I should consider surgery or wait for a miraculous healing. The closest I had come to anything surgery related was through watching shows like Grey's

Anatomy. I loved the scenes filmed in the Operating Room—they stirred curiosity and excitement in me that I didn't even know I had—but in reality, I feared the idea of having surgery. The pacing back and forth turned from hours to weeks to months until it was too late. Just like any storm, COVID-19 caused collateral damage.

Physical businesses closed, corporations and educational institutions switched to online, and many hospitals closed their doors to people who were not COVID-19 patients. My opportunity to access was slammed in my face. What this meant for me was that I was not able to get the surgery, medication, or even see my doctor. As these opportunities were swept away, I found myself turning to my closest friends and family for support. It was at that point that I realized how destructive being surrounded by people, yet still feeling alone, can be. Some people just didn't know how to support me. I saw friends disappear, some stopped talking to me out of fear of saying the wrong thing; and some, well, treated it like a trend and moved on. The rest of them became my pillars.

I was left wondering:

# WHO ENCOURAGES THE ENCOURAGER?

# WHO CHECKS UP ON THE FRIEND THAT ALWAYS CHECKS UP ON OTHERS?

It was in one of the most difficult and darkest seasons of my life that the revelation for this book came. Writing this book has not been easy. I thought: "No one can tell my story better than me". On August 11th, 2020, I finally had the surgery. 8 months after the initial diagnosis. During recovery, I spent days lying in bed because that was all I could do. Recovering from the surgery was no walk in the park. Trying to get back on my feet turned into this slow, painstaking journey where every step felt like a hard-earned victory over the toll my body had taken. You know, the kind of triumph that makes you appreciate the resilience we all have tucked away inside us. Putting one foot in front of the other wasn't just a physical thing; it was a daily reminder of the grit it takes to bounce back. Nights were marked by restlessness and discomfort, as my body grappled with the aftermath of the surgical intervention. Some nights, I found myself just lying there, staring at the ceiling, begging for the sweet relief of sleep. And then there were mornings where my win for the day was basically surviving the night. Every night became a new page in this complicated story of healing, each one with its own mix of struggles and small triumphs.

A few weeks later, I would spend the little energy I had, trying to scramble together words to form content for my social media platforms. After months of being less active due to my health challenges, I was eager to get back! I felt like I was missing out. For months behind the scenes, I went through one of the toughest battles in my life. Yet, on stage, I was producing, performing, and presenting. I used to think that if everything looks somewhat perfect from the outside, then it must be true within. It must be. We see this with Instagram and other social media platforms where we so easily compare ourselves based on how people present themselves on their platforms.

[i]An article by Penn Medicine states that, "Increasingly, young adolescents hold unrealistic expectations on what they should own, how they should look, or what they need to achieve, which is linked to higher rates of anxiety."

I had a firsthand experience of this. Not from comparing myself to others, but from the perspective of wearing a costume to trick the crowd.

I believe that all that glitters is not gold, and what I've found is that too many things glitter online, but they are not gold. Gold must go through a long, complex process of crushing and refining to become what we so easily marvel at today. I learned that when we strive for perfection or a perverse state of success, you throw away the process that is so necessary to get to the desired product. You can go through life believing perfectionism is the goal, only to later realize that it is the problem.

MANY OF US BECOME IMMUNE TO PAIN MEDICATION
BECAUSE PAIN BECOMES OUR MEDICATION.

It becomes what defines us, defiles us, and darkens our path. At least, that was my story. I had to learn to pivot my perspective, gain stewardship, and use leverage, to get through the most difficult parts of it. By shifting our perspective, we grant yourself the freedom to look at your challenges, sorrows, and difficulties from a vantage point beyond that of a victim. Once we see things differently, we can steward the rain within the storm by collecting, storing, and processing all the stories and experiences you have been through. Finally, we leverage each drop of rain to transform our struggles into successes, pains into purpose, and hardships into healing. It's much deeper than finding the silver lining.

I found it difficult to write about the emotional aspects of my experiences. I became demotivated as I reached the halfway point of this book because I knew something was missing. I came to realize that my heart was hardened towards much of what I had gone through, so I had become emotionally detached from those experiences. Writing this book was tough because I knew I had to recall past experiences but also travel back to those times in my life. I had to presently feel what I was not able to fully feel in the past. There was a lot I could not see back then that I see now. It was during this reflection time that allowed me to cry, feel anger, laugh, appreciate the old and anticipate the new. Through my profile, you see me as a person who has lived in five different countries before the age of twenty-five. On the outside, you see a lucky girl, on the inside I feel a brewing storm. The relocation came with challenges of internal conflict, always anticipating change, never feeling rooted and having a temporary mindset. These were the seeds that kept me bound to my past. It takes self-awareness to discover truth and depth: through revelation, true feeling, and context.

## WHEN WE STUDY OUR PATTERNS AND BEHAVIORS, WE UPROOT TOXIC WEEDS AND WATER THE FLOURISHING PLANTS.

We must go through the refining process to know which is which. Over the years, people have been intrigued by certain parts of my story that I did not think would serve a purpose to anyone else. Now with the understanding and appreciation of what I have gone through, I know that it can help someone else, even if it is just a chapter. As you read on, you will see that just because someone carries life well, does not mean it is not heavy. This is my own story, my own rocky path that I have lived through, that I am sharing with you to learn from. I share my story to shine a light on the young person who had to relocate at a young age for a myriad of reasons, to the person running from their past, the person dealing with identity crisis and to the person who is facing health issues. I share my experiences to strengthen and encourage those who want to know how to keep their faith, those who are experiencing vulnerable seasons or have experienced culture shock. I share my knowledge to empower people who desire to learn more about how to be resourceful in times of struggle and adversity. My hope is that the process I went through, and the principles learned, will help you fight through whatever you are battling with, knowing that you will surely come out a victor. What is ordinary to me can be extraordinary in the lives of other people. I've learned to not take telling my story for granted, and therefore prohibiting someone from learning from my experience. There was not much advice I received growing up, a lot of my learnings came through trial and tribulation.

As you will read from my story, having a handful of tough experiences allowed me to really reflect on the important things in life. It was also through reflecting, that I was able to receive all that God wanted to give me. To be able to get to the root of a problem, we sometimes need to stop focusing on what happened, and start asking ourselves why it happened. That's where self-awareness begins.

As you receive my thoughts and reflect on your life, it is my hope that your life will be transformed from the inside out.

## About the Book Title

The word "bound" as a **noun** represents a territorial limit or a restriction.

The word "bound" as an **adjective** represents the destined or likelihood for something to take place.

Bound to be Boundless is the understanding that we are restricted to be without restriction, but we are also destined to be without limits. It does not discount or neglect the toxic environments and negative experiences we go through, rather processes them in a way that helps us maintain our light amid darkness. My mindset transformation came when I understood that my turbulent relocation journey landed me opportunities some could only dream of. My revelation came when I understood that my past has not been for me to suffer, but through it, I was able to receive salvation through Jesus Christ. My breakthrough came when I learned to tune my eyes to see the light on my darkest days. There are two sides to every story. We are both bound, to be boundless and bound to be boundless.

# BEYOND THE BORDERS

"Beyond the Borders" explores the limitless possibilities of transcending geographical and personal boundaries. This chapter delves into the power of breaking free from societal expectations and embracing diversity, leading to a newfound sense of freedom and growth. This chapter will provide tools to embrace change and step outside your comfort zones to discover the beauty of the unknown.

# 1 BEYOND THE BORDERS

## I BELIEVE THAT WHEN GOD CLOSES A DOOR, HE WILL OPEN A WINDOW.

Our experiences are what make us who we are. I was less than 2 years old when I moved away from my birthplace, Nigeria. Little did I know that this was just the beginning of my journey. I have the idea that struggles draw you back to push you even further than where you were before. I believe this because of the experiences I have gone through; any struggles and barriers I have been up against, God has been faithful and gracious, and has always provided another way.

Sometimes when we face hardships, we feel like there is no way out or that we are not good enough. I can attest to this as there have been many instances in my life where I have felt as if I was not able to move forward from the struggle that I was going through.

I used to live in Bayreuth, a small town in Bavaria, Germany, that was filled with museums, opera houses and beautiful ancient buildings. I remember my mum speaking to one of the teachers at my Kindergarten (Nursery), discussing my ability to start school. In Germany, you start Kindergarten when you are 3 years old. My birthday falls towards the end of October, but the school year traditionally commences in September, which is a full month before I would have reached the age of three. It became apparent that I might have to wait another year before starting school.

To my mum's surprise, the teacher recommended that I shouldn't wait, but instead start Kindergarten at the age of 2 because I was a "bright" individual. My teacher would commend me, saying "Wunderbar", "Du bist sehr intelligent" (meaning "Wonderful" and "You are very intelligent"). My parents and other family members would praise me. Ever since knowing that I got admitted to kindergarten, earlier than all my friends, I became motivated to learn to read and write better. With German not being my parents' first language, they would always try to speak German in the house. As I was a very talkative child, they would correct me when I would use the wrong word or phrase. So, from a young age I was already aware of literature.

The transition from my early years in Germany to my move to Scotland marked a significant shift in my life. In Germany, my educational journey began in primary school (Grundschule), where I found myself at an advantage as the youngest in my class. It was during this period that the German educational system mandated the learning of cursive writing (Schreibschrift). I remember countless hours spent at our old wooden desks, diligently copying sentences in the prescribed font.

Then came the pivotal moment when my parents sat me down to announce our move to Scotland. As a young child, I struggled to comprehend the enormity of this change. I had no concept of Scotland's location or what lay ahead; all I knew was that I was leaving behind the familiarity of my friends and family. It was a journey into the unknown, a place teeming with strangers, unfamiliar languages, and a world that felt entirely different.

Upon arriving in Edinburgh, Scotland, the contrast between this bustling city and the tranquil Bavarian town of my upbringing was stark. My first year in the United Kingdom proved to be quite challenging. I found myself placed in an English as a Second Language (ESL) class, primarily because my proficiency in English was limited, and I predominantly spoke German.

It was within this ESL class that I first began learning how to read books, and the absence of German speakers in my new community served as a catalyst for rapidly acquiring fluency in English. However, my early years in the UK were marred by incidents of racism. I faced the arduous task of explaining to my peers that I had moved from Germany, yet I was of Nigerian descent. Many found it difficult to grasp this concept, leading to judgment and a barrage of questions about when I would return to my supposed home in Germany. Some classmates even questioned why I was in "their" country.

One unforgettable and deeply hurtful incident involved a

classmate labeling me a "Black Nazi." The sheer ignorance and disdain behind that remark brought me to tears and nearly drove me to the point of refusing to return to school. Such moments of bigotry and misunderstanding made me feel ashamed of having moved from Germany and identifying as German.

The prevailing perceptions about Germans, often entangled with historical events such as Hitler and the Holocaust, coupled with the perceived aggressiveness of the German language, as well as the stereotype of most Germans being white, had a significant impact on my family's experiences. Even the Germans we encountered in Edinburgh seemed hesitant to openly acknowledge their German roots or to speak the language. The weight of these stereotypes and a desire to blend in ultimately drove me to distance myself from my German identity. I started avoiding German TV shows, music, and even speaking the language at home in a bid to assimilate.

My sister who is 2 years older than me, faced a similar but more dramatic experience as she schooled in Nigeria, Germany, Scotland, and America. I asked her what she thought about her journey, and she told me that "Although my struggle was difficult, being able to adapt the way I did and especially being brought up multilingual, encouraged me to pursue a major in International Business and a minor in German." Looking back, I can say that the journey has been a profitable one for myself and my family.

The barriers that I faced relocating from one country to another certainly discouraged me. The biggest barrier was moving to America and attending an American high school for the first time. I started school as a senior. Having to cram 3 years of US history classes into 1 year, getting used to the transition from having little homework to 4-5 hours of homework every night and dealing with the stressful process of college applications and standardized testing made me feel as if I was not on the right path. Although when I reflect and look back at everything now, I realize that if God had let me follow a different path, my life would have been completely different and not necessarily better than it is now. I realize that if God had let me follow a different path such as finishing my high school year in the UK, my life might have led me to live a life of stagnancy, conforming to the mundane patterns of my comfort zone. I wouldn't have been challenged to break out of the shell that I had gotten so used to.

When my dad accepted his job in the US, I had to make the decision to either move to the US with him and my brother, or to finish high school in the UK and potentially pursue my degree there. At just 16, this choice weighed heavily on my young shoulders. And although there were times when I second-guessed my decision, I've grown to realize that the United States brought forth a wealth of opportunities that allowed me to truly embrace the potential of my future. The job ecosystem is more diverse, opportunities for personal growth abound, and the existence of financial capital was something that Scotland could not compete with. At the end of the day, every decision is a learning experience.

## Greatest Resistance

The greatest resistance often hides in the most unexpected places, and for me, it was nestled in the curious realm of bilingualism. The idea of raising bilingual children had been a topic of fascination and debate in many circles. Articles extolled the cognitive advantages of being both a bilingual child and senior, emphasizing the profound impact that bilingualism could have on one's life. As I delved into an article titled "Raising Bilingual Children," it struck a chord with me.

The authors spoke of how understanding a message in one language could be challenging if the other language consistently interfered, and this resonated with my experiences. My journey into the world of bilingualism had begun when I spent a year at my first primary school in Scotland. It was a year that revolved around endless encounters with books featuring the adventures of "Biff, Chip, and Kipper," characters from Oxford Reading Tree's publications designed to teach children to read English. Understandably, I faced my share of struggles during my initial year in this English-speaking country.

In my young mind, the boundaries between English and German often blurred. I found myself seamlessly mixing both languages, not only within my thoughts but also in my spoken words. During English class, I'd inadvertently declare, "Ich bin fine," and while tackling math problems, I'd count in a bizarre hybrid manner, "eins, zwei, drei, four, five."

Rosenberg's study, which explored the importance of learning a different language and growing up bilingual, emphasized the idea that consistency was the key to navigating this linguistic journey. She explained that if languages were mixed in the same conversation, young children might struggle to separate vocabulary and grammar into the appropriate language. In such cases, the child might end up learning the "mixed" language as a unique hybrid tongue. As I read these words, I couldn't help but draw parallels to my own linguistic evolution.

The experience of growing up bilingual is a unique journey, marked by its own set of challenges and triumphs. It is a testament to the adaptability of the human mind and the complexity of our ability to communicate. In the years that followed, my journey beyond the borders of language continued to shape not only my identity but also my perspective on the world. It was a journey that would lead me to discover the true power of embracing diversity and transcending linguistic boundaries.

# RECEIVE AND REFLECT - COMPARISON

**My thoughts:**
Comparison isn't just about what someone else possesses; it's often about how they navigate and achieve things with what they've got. It's a disservice to yourself to stack your journey and story against someone else's. The key is to stay focused on your purpose, and when you're truly engaged in your own path, comparison loses its power to distract.

Simply put, if we mind our own business and run with the grace tailor-made for our journey, we emerge victorious every time. Success isn't about coveting someone else's grass; it's about tending to our own and watching it flourish. By embracing our unique narrative, acknowledging the journey behind us, and eagerly anticipating what lies ahead, we not only appreciate our own story but also rise to the levels of those we admire.

---

**Self-reflection questions:**
- How do I balance the different parts of my multicultural identity?

- Think about a time when you had to adjust to a new culture. How did I handle the change, and what helped me adapt?

---

# THE FIGHT OF THE EXTERNAL

---

"The Fight of the External," explores the struggle that many individuals face when trying to control their external circumstances. Whether it's a difficult boss, financial stress, or health issues, it can be easy to become consumed by external events and let them dictate our happiness and well-being.

# 2 THE FIGHT OF THE EXTERNAL

"Despite your intelligence, your silence won't get you
very far."

A teacher from my second primary school in Scotland knelt
to my level and searched my eyes for understanding. Not
finding what she was looking for, she repeated "You can't
get very far." I couldn't quite put my finger on what her
intention was. To attack or to assist. Scottish people are
known to be blunt and raw. They will call a spade a spade.
I was singled out in class, called out in front of the other
students, and all I wanted to do was bury my head in the

table. As if being the only black student, with nappy hair, unfamiliar clothes, and a mixture of a Nigerian/German accent wasn't alarming enough. I looked around the classroom of stone-cold faces as I was blasted with hurtful words disguised as helpful advice. I felt cold inside and alone on the outside. I wanted to be known and applauded for my intelligence, but I was known and ridiculed for my silence, despite my intelligence. Relocating to a new country at such a tender age, I didn't know how people would respond to my accent, personality, and presence, so I made the choice to keep quiet and work hard.

I'm not alone in feeling this way. In her article, the Idea of Home, Natasha Malpani Oswal[ii] shares, "Keep your head down, and work hard. Don't attract any attention. You should be grateful to be here."

I did not know what to believe anymore. Keeping my head down became the exact action that attracted more attention. As this was a few years after relocating to Scotland, I needed to find a way to assimilate to the culture. I was tired of being the "different" one and just wanted to fit in. From my observation, it seemed like most of the class were class clowns and disruptors, carrying all the confidence in the world. I wanted to be like them. More vocal and more confident. I thought the end justified the means, but I was wrong.

Yes, I became more vocal in class, but I also became the student that would talk back at teachers, have conversations during class, and make fun of other students. I did this to fit in, but my actions resulted in me no longer doing well in class. Though I gained more friends on the "cool" side, I lost the respect of teachers because of my newly developed behavior. I turned into a person I couldn't recognize anymore. I knew that this was not me. I am not one to disrespect my elders and make fun of other students. *I* used to be the student that others would make fun of. Though the shoe was on the other foot, it was an uncomfortable fit. I thought this is what it meant to be 'different'. I thought that this is what my headteacher was *telling* me to do. My forceful desire to be different almost became my demise. I started to act differently, look different and even speak differently. It wasn't nature, I was nurturing toxic weeds.

Trying to assimilate to the culture led me to falling into the wrong crowd.

## WHEN YOU DON'T KNOW WHO YOU ARE INTERNALLY, YOU WILL ACCEPT EVERYTHING AND ANYTHING FROM THE OUTSIDE.

By not willing to fight the external, I was already living a defeated life. I had to make a choice. I had to understand whether it was the presence of something or the lack of something that was at the root of my behavior and actions. It was a risk I had to take to uproot those toxic weeds. I had to decide whether to operate from a place of attacking life through the lens of insecurity or defending my identity, being who I knew deep down to be true. It was a battle of staying in the comfort of the friends that could delay my destiny or stepping out to find new friends that would help my destiny. I valued direction, and though I had been led astray, I knew it was more important to know where I was going than to get there quickly.

Having switched between being the "quiet Blessing", "cool Blessing" and somewhere in between – I realized I had no idea who I was. I was trying to figure out my identity, by focusing on my image. Only to realize that my image was merely what I wanted people to see, but my identity is who I really was. When I compared myself to others, for the sake of assimilating, it stole my identity. Left with nothing, I was wandering a dark and frightening world, trying to place my identity in external things. The world around me was always going to change, and if I continued in the way I did, I would lose the fight of the external. I always felt like an outsider – not being Nigerian enough, German enough and *definitely* not Scottish enough. I didn't know where I belonged - *if* I belonged.

Natasha Malpani Oswal, who grew up in India, and lived in England before moving to America, explores the same immigrant narrative that supports my reality stating, "Living in a country shapes your personality, interests, and relationships. I've had to start over from scratch so many times, that I can barely remember who I used to be."[iii]

## EMBRACING WHO I WAS AND WHERE I CAME FROM OPENED MORE DOORS FOR ME THAN PRETENDING TO BE WHO I WAS NOT.

By embracing and celebrating my background, I was able to find and build a diverse group of friends. I had a friend from New Zealand, one who danced, one who was the class clown, one who was artistic, the list could go on. The fusion of friends and understanding of identity was in my favor because I gave up the fight of external realities and gave into my internal development. Even my complexities have complimented my calling as I can identify myself with different people, and different parts of the world.

Who told you that you were not good enough? It is not every voice you hear that you give value to. I valued observation so much that I would look too far ahead at what other people were doing, that I missed out on what I had right under my nose. As I learned to steward what I had right in front of me, I saw that the grass became greener where I watered it. That same grass produced the oxygen for me to breathe, and enabled me to find my voice and make my presence known in every room I found myself in.

## Coming to America

As I walked up the stairs to enter the security section of the airport, my friends from high school jumped out to surprise me one last time. The experience was so overwhelming and emotional that I waited until I was sitting in the window seat of the plane, to let my emotions reveal themselves. I could not believe that it was finally happening. There I was, sitting on a plane, with a one-way ticket to what I knew as the land of opportunity. I remember staring out of the window, as the plane flew past the land I had come to accept as 'home'.

The first time I touched foot in America was the first time I lost touch with the life I had envisioned for myself. Everything was about to change, and it was a feeling I could not shake off. It was my new reality.

I always saw America as a country where I would visit temporarily, a country that I would go to for a holiday, but not one that I would stay in permanently. This mindset contaminated my criticism of the country, which led me to filtering everything through a lens of victimhood. Relocating to America in my senior year of high school was one of the most difficult decisions I had to make. Not only did I have to think about my family's situation, but I also had to think about my future. At the time, I did not realize that my family's situation would affect my future. As the middle child in my family, I was in an inconvenient position compared to my siblings. I wouldn't say it was new. As the middle child, I was also the only child born in Nigeria, whereas my older sister and younger brother were born in Germany. Think about that for a second. For me, moving to America meant leaving family and friendships that have developed over 10 years of living in Scotland. It meant having to forget all the planning I did. It meant having to leave behind my friends, my plans, my dreams, you name it.

My first year in America and last year in high school was one that I will never forget. Not only did it change my life, but it also challenged my perspective. I remember being so shocked at the fact that students get hours upon hours of homework in high school. It was so different, in the sense that at most, students get a total of 1 hour of homework after school. I did not have many friends at school. Not many seniors actually knew that I was a senior. As frustrating as it was, high schools in the United States have a policy in which one must complete certain classes to graduate. In the space of a year, I had to take a biology class as well as 3 history classes that are usually spaced out across 3 years. I started to question what purpose moving to the United States could potentially birth. I felt like I was living life on autopilot. I convinced myself that I had made the wrong decision.

The more I convinced myself, the more I was blinded to see the opportunities that were right in front of me. Something I realized is that it was me holding the blinds in front of my eyes. It was not that the resources and opportunities were not there, the problem was my inability to be resourceful. It was my inability to see beyond my circumstance. It was the pain that became my medication. On my high school graduation day, I was nowhere to be found. As the school year came to an end and graduation came near, I was physically, mentally, and emotionally exhausted. It was a year that I will never forget. It was an experience that I needed to escape. So, I did just that. On the day of my graduation, I was on a plane back to Scotland. My experience was so bad that I became numb to celebrating what may have been the most exhausting year, but also the year that I had seen the most development.

The first time I touched foot in Scotland after leaving, I suddenly felt like I could breathe again. It was as if, all throughout my senior year of high school, I had been holding my breath. Though not literally, I thought that the intensity of the experience would kill me, but instead it gave life to a Blessing that I had never seen before. The few months I spent in Scotland for the summer allowed me to reflect and refresh. As I learned to appreciate the journey I had gone through, I also started to anticipate the new season.

My summer was filled with new memories, fun activities, and unexpected questions. Friends, family, and acquaintances would start to prod and question the decisions I was making. The most frequent question was, "Why would you study in the United States, when you could get free education in Scotland?" That question became the turning point in my journey, but I did not know it at the time. I would respond with a weak laugh that masked my insecurity and a shrug that heightened my anxiety. I started to question the decision myself. To everyone, it seemed like a no-brainer, but they did not know that this was the next piece of the puzzle that God was going to use to perfect his masterpiece.

Coming back to the United States, sitting on the same plane that flew me out of my comfort zone and delivered me in the wilderness, I started to feel like I was given another chance. That this time, when I landed in the United States, I came with a new identity, less baggage, and a destination that would reveal my destiny. On that day, a year after I permanently relocated to the United States, I promised myself that I would live my life from a place of thriving, not merely surviving. I have come to realize that I was not necessarily *only* tired because of the physical, emotional, and mental stress, but because I was actively fighting against seeing things a different way. It was time to loosen the shackles and grab the freedom that so many had talked of.

## Fight or flight

I'm sorry you feel discouraged. I'm sorry you've had thoughts of giving up. I'm sorry that you have fallen victim to a cycle of unfortunate events. I'm sorry that your fear and anxiety has become the norm. I'm sorry that you have been in a perpetual state of survival mode. I'm sorry that you have been waiting for an answer, breakthrough, change, for years and years. Let go of the guilt you carry for your perceived role in your struggles. Forgive yourself for accusing God of not loving you. I'm sorry that you have had to question God's purpose for your life as you wait in the storm. I'm sorry that you've thought of hurting yourself. I'm sorry that people have left, hurt, (ab)used you. I'm sorry that you have become desensitized to the encouragement of your friends, family, and the word of God. I'm sorry that all of this has caused you to succumb to this way of life. without hope for a better future.

In Isaiah 55 we hear about how God's thoughts are higher than ours, that His ways are better than ours and His plans are bigger than ours. It's difficult to comprehend it with our human mind. The Creator is greater than His creation. God thinks a thought, speaks the Word and whatever it is, it happens. God's ways are beyond the comprehension of man. God is all knowing. He knows all because everything is part of His plan. And because everything is part of His plan, we must remind ourselves that just because we have faced bad days/weeks/months/years, does not mean that your life can't change in an instant when God speaks.

As I write this, I can't help but think back to the tiring 2-and-a-half-year journey I had been on with my health. To say it was difficult is an understatement. So, this particular message is for the person who is tired. Tired of fighting, tired of hoping for a change, tired of crying out to God, tired of waiting. I see you. Please don't give up. Please don't harden your heart. With all the no's you have received, please continue to wait, as long as it may take, all you need is one yes.

# RECEIVE AND REFLECT - PERSEVERANCE

**My thoughts:**

Navigating and implementing change is no small feat for those carrying the weight of the task. Perseverance, a quality born out of overcoming adversity, isn't cultivated in the midst of a trouble-free life. There was a time when I believed that perseverance could only be developed in the midst of a comfortable and smooth sailing life. However, I've come to understand that this trait emerges from experiences of stumbling and picking oneself up again. It's about the resilience found in standing tall after a fall, and the cumulative strength gained with each setback that equips individuals to thrive in the face of challenges. Amid various trials, one that stands out vividly is the period when I juggled classes and internships for three consecutive summers. Each summer brought its own waves of hopelessness and imposter syndrome, yet the experience from the previous summer served as a wellspring of strength for the next.

---

**Self-reflection questions:**

- What hurdles am I determined to conquer? Why?

- In reaching this point, what obstacles have I already triumphed over?

- Do specific habits or routines help me sustain perseverance?

---

# FREE BUT STILL BOUND

"Free but Still Bound" explores the concept of freedom and its limitations. Despite being free from external constraints, individuals may still be bound by internal fears, societal expectations, and past experiences. This chapter delves into the idea that true freedom lies in the ability to break free from these internal bounds and truly embrace one's own sense of liberation.

# 3 FREE BUT STILL BOUND

"I am surrounded by people, I fear no one".

This is the meaning of my surname. A powerful statement that encourages confidence and courage. In my quest for friends, being confident and courageous were two traits that were not so apparent in my senior year of high school in America. Here I was, roaming the packed hallways of my high school, entertaining myself with conflicting conversations in my head. The hallways were polluted with the laughter and conversations of students who seemed to have no care in the world. I could imagine the sound waves hitting off the stone-cold walls, with me as their next target. I could barely hear my own thoughts and that made it much lonelier. The air was filled with different smells that would either make me feel nauseous or nostalgic, depending on which hallway I walked down. I recognized some students who I had seen in my classes, and asked myself if I should stop and say hi to them. Luckily, before coming to America, I had watched too many American high school movies to know how such an interaction would turn out: become a weird loner or bullied for being new. For some reason, I never pictured myself as 'that girl'. Scouring the hallways of high school, hoping to meet the eyes of that one person, a new friend, that would make my journey less lonely.

As I travelled through the stereotypical popular kids, athletes, and everyone in between, I feared the thought of being labeled as the 'new', 'weird' or 'loner' kid. This fear became a shackle I carried with me wondering: Was everyone looking at me? Were they wondering why I kept aimlessly walking the hallways? Do they feel sorry for me? These questions fueled my adventure, as I anticipated finding the answers through the facial expressions of the students that littered the hallways. The more questions I had, the heavier the shackles became. I was burdened with worries. It came to a point where doing laps around my school was just my way of passing away the time, not necessarily searching for someone to sit with or talk to. When I did find the courage to find a place to sit down by myself, I looked to my friends in Scotland to fill the void.

All the friends I needed were in my pocket. With the touch of a button, I could free myself of thinking I was alone, but realized that whilst I was doing that, I was still bound to a fixed mentality. I was physically in America, but mentally in Scotland. In a way, I did experience a level of freedom when I spoke to my friends back home. It was the freedom to be myself because they knew who I was. With them, I was an unapologetic version of myself. In America, no one knew me, and that scared me. The blaring bell that signaled the end of lunch time, the school day and my daydreams, became the thing that I most looked forward to. It was as if the sound of the bell scared my anxiety away, and I could finally exhale, but only for so long until I would have to hold my breath again. It was the best part of my day, knowing I could finally go home, and not be subconsciously persecuted or pressured into making friends.

I valued being alone: it was a state allowing me to enjoy my own company and learn more about myself. At this point in my life, being alone was the main thing familiar and consistent to me. It was the world I grew up in, despite having lived in Nigeria, Germany, and Scotland before this point. I became someone who feared being surrounded by people. It was a choice I made and was content with because I convinced myself that my stay in America would only be temporary. What was the point of making new friends? As I continued in the cycle of roaming the hallways, I carried this fixed mindset with me. The fixed mindset became a shackle. Getting tighter and tighter. Restricting the way I thought, walked, and talked. The next day would come, introducing another cycle of anxious thoughts, and mundane routine. I sat in these classes with 99% freshmen, the 1% being myself, the only senior. It was another experience that made me feel more isolated. An article about 'Problems Faced by International Students' mentions how these challenges, ". . . results in isolation, emotional issues, and anxiety that thus affects academic performance and capability." Being the 1% was not new to me. I was the 1% as the only black student in my Kindergarten class in Germany . I was the 1% as the only German speaker in my classes in Scotland. Sitting in a crowded classroom and feeling like I was invisible was a new feeling I could not shake off.

## INSTEAD OF TRYING TO FIGHT THE FEELING, I DECIDED TO WEAR THE CLOAK OF INVISIBILITY WITH CONFIDENCE.

I was under the illusion of freedom. This was one of the first appearances of the traits that come from my surname. My actions followed my dark thoughts as I stopped raising my hand in class and instead used that hand to figuratively cover my mouth and stop myself from speaking. Physically and mentally, I sank to the back of the class and became a self-imposed enigma.

Checking myself back into victimhood allowed me to not only experience the default but explore the destined path.

The very thing I looked down on, I could use to my advantage. Every day, for most of the school day, I was surrounded by eager freshmen who were open to making new friends too. They were in the same boat as me, the only difference was I allowed my title as a senior to hold me back from steering the boat, so I ended up sinking where they were thriving. I grabbed onto a lifeline that pushed me to identify at least one person in each class who seemed interesting. Though I was still anxious when starting conversations in person, I held on to what I knew best at the time—online communication. Holding tightly to this new revelation, I rushed home, turned to Facebook and started recalling the unique students, through months of observation, I could get used to replacing with "my friend." With my research hat on, I started learning more about the person and through finding similar interests, I sent them a message, asking if we could hang out during lunch one day. At this point, there was nothing to lose.

I worried they probably would not recognize me in the hallway anyway, but to my surprise my hesitant request was met with a humbling response. I may not have found a new friend, but I had finally found someone to spend my lunch hour with. This time, as I scoured the hallway, I had the goal of finding the person I had reached out to, knowing that they saved a spot for me. As we spent lunch sharing experiences, laughs and opinions, I felt like I had been resuscitated. I felt free to believe better days were ahead. I was finally starting to warm up to the idea of being surrounded by someone and being at ease. The figurative ecstasy quickly wore off as this only lasted for a few days. They had other friends to get back to, so my few memorable lunch hours became merely one-offs.

A fresh flood of questions invaded me as my inner conflict grew, wanting to swallow me whole. I started to sink deeper than I had before. I could not understand why what seemed like a miraculous lifeline was instead a weight dragging me deeper into the unknown. It was like people were laughing at me drowning. I started to laugh at myself too, thinking I could change the very world I was so used to. Who was I to create such a change? Were they hanging out with me out of pity? I wanted to give up. I was already so close to the bottom. The scary thing about drowning is when you drown, your body goes into survival mode, causing you to kick, scream, do anything that will allow you to get to the surface. What many do not know is these very actions can also be the cause of why you sink deeper and deeper.

At this moment, I knew I had to risk it because the remainder of my high school journey depended on it. It was a decision that threw me so far out of my comfort zone I didn't know if I was going to be able handle it. To continue being able to spend my lunch hour with people in my classes, I had to continually find the courage to ask them again and again. At this point, I actualized the two traits attached to my surname. Though my actions showed otherwise, my heart valued community too much to just let it slip out of my hand. You could say it was the Nigerian in me.

I learned I was trying to run, but the shackles of my identity crisis were causing me to fall, again and again. It was my choice to keep picking myself up and continue running that was going to change anything on the outside. Long lasting change could only come from having the confidence and courage to completely lose the shackles stopping me from making new friends, creating new experiences, and planning a fulfilling future.

These shackles convinced me I was better on my own because they were familiar. These shackles convinced me I was not interesting enough to be known or seen by anyone because I did not even know who I was. These shackles convinced me I was comfortable where I was: the shackles were there when others were not. These shackles were lies gripping me, but they didn't have to hold me back. These shackles were part of my identity I had to let go of, to experience boundless freedom, no shackles attached.

For the longest time, I had been battling with my mind, but as I began to think greater than how I felt, things started to change. Eventually, I was able to open myself up to making new friends with freshmen and seniors. I spent my lunch breaks talking and laughing with my newfound friends. Engaging with them was an active and deliberate decision I had to make each day. Freeing myself from the shackles that used to keep me in the familiar past, allowed me to give

America another chance by staying for university. By staying, I was giving myself another chance to learn from my old patterns and toxic behaviors, even as I anticipated new challenges ahead. Due to how I chose to see the situation, a blessing emerged from carrying the burden.

FREEDOM WAS A CHOICE. IT WAS DOWN TO MY MINDSET TO CHOOSE THE KEY AND UNLOCK THE SHACKLES.

**That night in that desolate place.**

As I sat there, looking around this empty hall filled with people, I couldn't help but reflect on the ironies that life often presents. In the pursuit of freedom and personal liberation, I had found myself in a place that, on the surface, appeared to be the epitome of confinement—a psychiatric ward.

The rooms, minimally furnished with functional pieces, echo with a quiet that somehow amplifies the internal battles of those inside. Beds are neatly made, linens crips, offering a semblance of order in what feels like a whirlwind of emotions. It's intentional, the lack of personal touch, a way to keep things simple and safe. We all wore the same simple robe – a great equalizer that turned everyone into a shared canvas of vulnerability. Imagine a place where your phone, the little trinkets of jewelry you wear, even the comforting hold of a hairband, all had to stay outside. It was like shedding layers of identity at the door. Stripped of our everyday stuff, we were left with just ourselves, and each other.

The sterile, fluorescent-lit corridors, the controlled routines, and the watchful eyes of the staff could easily have convinced anyone that this was a place of restriction. It was a space where personal autonomy appeared to be temporarily revoked, where the weight of one's own limitations hung heavily in the air. But there was more to this place than met the eye. It was in this very setting that I would come to understand the essence of being "bound to be boundless." The title of this chapter epitomized the intricate dance between constraint and liberation that I experienced during my time in the psychiatric ward.

In those moments, as I sat in that hall filled with people who were on their own unique journeys of self-discovery, I came to appreciate the significance of my circumstances. In this shared space, the boundaries that separated us were not the traditional walls of a psychiatric facility; they were the invisible barriers we had built around our own minds and hearts. The phrase "bound to be boundless" took on a new meaning as I navigated the psych ward's daily routines and listened to late-night conversations with fellow residents (to put it nicely). We were a diverse group, each with our own stories and struggles, but we all shared the vulnerability that comes from confronting our own minds and emotions.

The paradox lies in the realization that, while our circumstances may have temporarily bound us within the walls of the ward, the experience allowed us to explore the boundless aspects of our humanity. We were free from the judgments of the outside world, free from the masks we wore to conform to societal expectations. In this space, we had nothing to lose because we had already relinquished our facades and pretenses. In the emptiness of that sterile environment, I discovered something extraordinary—self-awareness, empathy, and the courage to confront my own limitations. I was free to delve into the depths of my emotions, to confront my inner demons, and to heal. No phone. No bible. I remember having to rely on what I remembered of scripture, to encourage myself. No hair bands. No jewelry. No shoes. Not even a bathroom mirror to look at yourself.

Amidst this journey, I discovered that the key to securing release from the psychiatric ward was to demonstrate a profound self-awareness and a readiness to confront the inner demons that had tethered us. It was a truly extraordinary notion—that the route to freedom lay in our capacity to comprehend and embrace the intricacies of our own existence.

As the clinical team assessed not just our symptoms but also our readiness to re-enter the world outside, they examined our stability, our treatment plans, the safety of our chosen environments, the presence of a support system, and the efficacy of our coping strategies. It was a process that prioritized not just our safety, but our empowerment. It was a process that recognized that genuine freedom doesn't only come from escaping external confines, but from transcending the limits we place upon ourselves.

In the ward, I had no choice but to learn that I could be free even when bound.

In the world, I had no choice but to rid the idea that I can be free but still bound.

# RECEIVE AND REFLECT - FAITH

**My thoughts:**
Growing up, I used to always hear the testimonies and stories of those who grew up in church their entire life or grew up in a Christian home. Through my eyes, they were the "model" Christian's, the perfect ones. It wasn't until a few years after I was saved, that I had to realize that no one is perfect, even a Christian. Especially a Christian. Each Christian is travelling their own, personal journey with God and in their faith. It will look different for everyone, and in different seasons but it's important to hold onto the fact that there is grace for a given race. Meaning, one doesn't need to look to the right or left of them, there is no competing with Christianity. Parents can't force it. Knowing God and accepting Him, is a promise that happens between you and Him only.

---

**Self-reflection questions:**
- How has my perception of faith transformed throughout my life's journey?

- What significance does my personal journey with God hold for me, and which aspects of it carry the most importance in my life?

- What do I perceive as my life's purpose and mission?

---

55

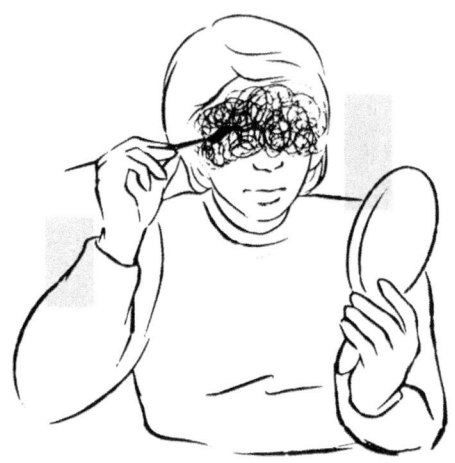

# SHARDS OF A BROKEN REFLECTION

"Shards of a Broken Reflection" delves into the shattered pieces of our past and how they shape our present selves. I explore the idea that despite the fractures and cracks in our lives, we can still transcend them and find freedom and wholeness. The shattered pieces of our past can be daunting, but they do not have to define us.

# 4 SHARDS OF A BROKEN REFLECTION

## The first punch that broke the mirror

*"Where are you really from?*

*What are you doing here?*

*When are you going back?"*

These were the 3 questions that my family would be asked whenever meeting someone new in Germany. Questions that seemed harmless and subtle, were the exact reflection of Germany's state of racism at the time. Germans would call it a conversation. I would call it an interrogation. As I stood beside my parents, I could tell that their mere presence caused Germans to fear. How could one's presence dictate such an atmosphere, yet they were still so inferior? From the little I could understand from the questions, I concluded that a black person living in Germany was always assumed to be a foreigner, a fraud and only a temporary resident. I was convinced that being black meant that you could not be German. As the only black student in my kindergarten classes and on the playground, I stood out like a sore thumb. There I was, a 5-year-old black girl with nappy hair, Nigerian native wear, and a German accent. The start of the complexity of my complexion. A sight to see, yet one so many avoided.

One day I ran home from school, crying to my dad because I was made fun of for my skin color. My skin was known as "chocolate skin" and to them, it was ugly and dirty. I remember being comforted by my dad who encouraged me that my skin was beautiful. It was still hard to believe. To have felt so uncomfortable in my own skin meant that I had questioned all the unique features that made me, me. I cried, not because the other kids pointed out the fact that I was black, but because I started to think that being black was wrong. Looking in the mirror, I was brought to only see what people thought of me. This was the first punch that broke the mirror, distorting my reflection.

## Picking up the pieces

Relocating to Scotland threw me into a relapse of questioning my appearance. Not much changed, I was still a black girl in a predominantly white town, city, and country. The only difference was that now, I spoke German in a non-German speaking country. An added complexity. One thing after another, I had more reasons to feel ugly and unimpressive. My classmates also did not allow me to forget it. From statements like "go back to your country" and "black nazi," I was constantly reminded that who I was, was not accepted. It was during these experiences that I started to entertain the thought of altering my physical appearance. When I introduced doubt into my circumstance, I ended up focusing on what I did not have, rather than what I did.

The gap between my two front teeth became the brunt of my insecurity. I was known as "the London look" girl – a term used to describe women with a gap between their two front teeth. It was not a compliment. People would make fun of the look by placing a chocolate chip between their two front teeth or using a black marker to create the illusion. After a day of facing the bullies, I would spend hours at night trying to squeeze my two front teeth together, in hopes that I could fix it. Then came features such as my nose, ears, and lips. It was an unfortunate mix between thinking that my nose was too flat, my ears were too small, and my lips were too big. Nothing about me was good enough. I had too many options for people to make fun of and too few features I embraced. I remember experimenting with various ways to make myself look different, and in doing so, I was only hurting myself. I was so desperate and the world around me was getting impatient. My culture assimilation came with a cost. One that was too expensive to pay. This was the second punch that shattered the mirror into thousands of tiny shards.

Too many times, I gave people or situations permission to take those shards. What I found was that I was left with an even more distorted view of myself. Through the relationships and negative experiences, I placed so much of my identity in, when the shards fell off, I no longer knew who I was. I no longer recognized who was in the mirror. That is the thing about negative thoughts and experiences, they try to get us to compare ourselves and focus on ability and outward appearance. Every chance I got, I would stand in front of a mirror looking at my appearance and physical stature and hating what I saw. My trauma, past hurts, identity crisis, and deep loneliness became the reflection of every mirror that I looked into. It was not me that I was looking at. It was a distorted view of what I went through. Sometimes it is difficult to even tell the difference. As I looked into my reflection, I could see all the physical and emotional scars that had defined me for so long. The voices that convinced me that my 'superficial' would always be better than the 'original.' The images I saw online made fun of people who looked like me. Living in Germany and Scotland, as an African, forced me to have to embrace all the features that made me different from those I was surrounded by. In the midst of broken glass, I had to pick the pieces up and figure out how to place things back together.

# JUST BECAUSE SOMETHING IS BROKEN, DOES NOT MEAN THAT IT IS PERMANENTLY DAMAGED.

Sometimes it is the broken pieces that create a masterpiece. The beauty is that the masterpiece was there all along. Growing up in a Nigerian household, I was no stranger to the rich tapestry of culture, traditions, and customs that defined our heritage. But it was not until I stepped beyond the familiar confines of my home and ventured into the broader Nigerian community that I began to grapple with a profound sense of not being "Nigerian enough."

As I interacted with Nigerians from various backgrounds, I became acutely aware of the diverse tapestry of identities that make up the Nigerian diaspora. Each person brought their own unique stories, traditions, and perspectives, and my own upbringing sometimes felt like a fragment in this intricate mosaic.

The sense of not being Nigerian enough weighed on me. I could not help but compare myself to others, particularly those who had grown up in Nigeria or had more direct exposure to our culture. Fitting in seemed to be an elusive goal, a mirage that shimmered tantalizingly on the horizon but remained just out of reach. Even if I managed to blend in or adopt certain customs, it was as if something intangible separated me from being truly authentic in the eyes of those who had always been immersed in the culture.

This struggle to fit in stirred feelings of self-doubt and inadequacy. I questioned whether my identity as a Nigerian was valid and whether I had a place within the broader Nigerian community. It was a battle between the desire to honor my roots and the daunting realization that my experiences made me different, setting me apart from the traditional narrative of what it meant to be Nigerian.

The journey of coming to terms with not being "Nigerian enough" was a transformative one. I began to recognize that authenticity was not defined by how closely I adhered to cultural norms or traditions but by embracing my own unique blend of experiences and perspectives. It was a realization that being true to myself, and my personal journey was more important than conforming to external expectations.

In this way, I learned that fitting in would never be good enough because my authenticity was far more valuable. It was a lesson that extended beyond cultural identity, teaching me the importance of embracing my individuality in every aspect of life. While I continued to honor my Nigerian heritage, I also embraced the truth that I was more than the sum of cultural expectations, and that my identity was a complex, evolving narrative that deserved to be celebrated.

## Scared and Scarred

Sometimes the recovery can be more painful than the injury itself. In my case, my recovery was more painful than the surgery. When I had the opportunity to get surgery for my tumor, I was not thinking too much of the recovery process. If anything, I assumed the recovery would be smooth and seamless. I remembered visiting the doctor a week after the surgery. As I sat on the cold bench, awaiting the all-clear, the reality of my recovery dawned on me. As the doctor pulled off the medical gauze from the surgery location, I felt that something was missing. The tumor was removed, but I felt something else had left. It was the body that I came to embrace. There was a visible indent of where the tumor used to be, and a scar to commemorate the event. Though something was removed, I was still whole. Our bodies are constantly changing, whether it is intentional or unintentional. Regardless, when I started to introduce hope into my circumstance, I started to focus on what I did have. Life. My scars became evidence of what I had been through, and most importantly, what I overcame.

Though I say all of this, from experience, I know it's not easy. I know that it can take months, sometimes years to get to this point of optimism or revelation where you truly understand what has happened and what is currently happening. It takes time to talk positively to yourself. It takes practice to convince your mind that you will be okay. It is a habit you form. It's the mirror that you put together piece by piece, from the shards of your hope, confidence, and dreams that have been broken and dismantled too many times. It is this that will stand the test of time. I say all of this to say that it is okay to fear your scars, for they will not haunt you forever.

## To Like and to love

For over 21 years, I was unhappy in my own skin. I was frustrated by how I looked, spoke, walked, talked, you name it. The expectations around me to look a certain way were high, but my affirmations were low. Living in a constant state of identity crisis made me forget who I was. I was so unrecognizable that I started to allow others to dictate how I should look. Over the years, I had been looking at a broken reflection of myself. Each glass shard showed me a distorted view. It made me question, why do we undervalue ourselves and overvalue others? Sometimes I found myself appreciating so much of other people's journeys and appearances that it started to depreciate my value. To have been upset over what I did not have, wasted what I did have. I had to go through seasons of learning to like and then love myself. By being more intentional about learning more about myself, investigating my unique features and embracing them, I started to enjoy my own company and liked who I was becoming. Amid external realities, I had to learn to love my body for what it is and love myself for who I am.

It was through the brokenness that light was able to pour through. It was through the gaps that I was able to find fulfillment in the very things that made me, me. It was in the lack of representation of people that looked like me, that allowed me to know who I was and present myself at the level that God created me. As a man thinketh, so is he. Many times, what starts as a breakdown ends with a breakthrough. To like ourselves is to recognize and embrace the shards of a broken reflection. To love ourselves is to have the courage to piece together the shards to create a wholesome reflection.

# RECEIVE AND REFLECT - IDENTITY

## My thoughts:

Start from scratch, as if the slate is blank. Often, it's cluttered with the echoes of others' words and the imprints of our observations. In the pursuit of crafting an image, our true identity can fade into the background. While image is what we project, identity is the essence of who we truly are. Amid the effort to escape aspects of ourselves we dislike, our identity can be easily forgotten. Allocate time to delve into both your internal and external self—acknowledging both the commendable and the challenging. It's often the facets we may not admire that empower us to make a meaningful impact in the world. Embrace the entirety of your identity, for it is the authentic foundation from which your unique contributions can blossom.

---

**Self-reflection questions:**

- Do my projected image and authentic identity align consistently?

- In what manner has my past contributed to shaping my identity, and in what ways do I aspire to evolve or transform?

---

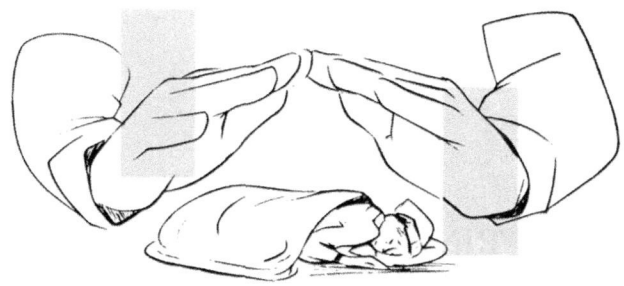

# THE PRINCIPLE OF PERSPECTIVE

"The Principle of Perspective" delves into the importance of viewing situations from multiple angles. It highlights the power of perspective in shaping our thoughts, emotions, and actions. Perspective is a choice, and with that choice comes the power to shape our lives and reach new levels of understanding and fulfillment.

# 5 THE PRINCIPLE OF PERSPECTIVE

## Perspective vs. Perception

Perception is what you interpret.

Perspective is the lens you see the world through.

I remember when I was sitting with my friends in high school, in Scotland, studying for our upcoming Math exam, when I received a phone call from my dad. I already knew the news he was going to share would be good or bad. As I listened to the tone of his voice, I knew what he was going to say. He shared the news that Princeton Theological Seminary had given him the job as a professor and that we would be moving to New Jersey in the United States. As my voice started to tremble because I was on the verge of crying, my friends anxiously looked at me as they did not understand what was happening. After I got off the phone, it took me a couple of minutes to recollect myself before I could tell them the good but also sad news. I told my friends that my dad received the job and that I would be moving to America in a couple of months. I was glad that they were happy for me, but I could also feel the sadness in their voices as they congratulated me.

At the time I could not comprehend what had happened and what was about to happen. I almost did not want it to be a reality. After moving from Germany, I already felt as if I had lost touch with all my friends and family that I had left there, and I certainly did not want that to happen in Scotland. I had three months to pack up ten years of my life spent in Scotland. This transition was the most difficult to deal with as I made many friends, established new relationships with people, became comfortable where I was and created so many memories. I was not ready to leave everything behind (previously, I had only visited America a few times on holiday, when I was much younger). Since the news, I found myself watching increasingly more American movies, YouTube videos about New Jersey and videos to try and get myself prepared for the new culture, spelling, pronunciations, accents, traditions, and education system.

In September 2015, I moved to Princeton, New Jersey. Never did I think that the next piece of my puzzle was going to be in the United States. Apart from the fact that English is spoken in both the United Kingdom and the United States, I did experience a huge culture shock. Even now, I still struggle to understand some accents. I still find myself using British slang such as saying "chips" instead of "fries," "cinema" instead of "movies," "trousers" instead of "pants," but I know that I do this on purpose. As much as I want to fit in society here, using British slang makes me feel more at home and different, but different in a good way. I always remember a birthday card that my best friend in Scotland sent to me back in 2015, it reads *"Dae ye mind a lang*

*lang time ago, when you were only wee...ye played at cowboys in the street and fitba in the park...the world has changed so much since then, in mony different ways. But I guess ye'll think back fondly tae those happy childhood days."* She specifically sent this to me just so that I would not forget my Scots language.

One of the first culture shocks that I experienced at Drexel University, was the housing and roommate situation. The idea that you are living away from home, sharing a room with someone that you do not know that well, sharing other utilities like bathroom and kitchen, with a whole floor of strangers, scared me. Another culture shock was making friends and learning about other people's experiences from different geographical locations with diverse backgrounds. It was both different and interesting to make friends this way. I tend to be homesick wherever I go. Now living in America, I miss my home in Edinburgh, Scotland. When I was living in Scotland, I missed my home in Bayreuth, Germany and when I was living in Germany, I missed my home in Lagos, Nigeria. Therefore, I experience homesickness in a slightly unique way from people who have only lived in one place. As well as still getting used to the way the American education system works, I feel disoriented sometimes, as the environment in high school is completely different from college. I am more independent, have many more responsibilities and identify as an adult. Owing to the multiple identities I now have, deriving from living and growing up within four different countries in the last twenty-two years, I identify Nigeria, Germany, Scotland, and the United States as home.

## The Principle of Perspective

Being an 'alien' in America is not easy. As an untraditional international student, I was not eligible for loans or scholarships because of my status. I struggled with how to reconcile being in America in the first place. It was never part of my plan. For my first one and a half years in college, I faced the struggle of being an international student. Many international students across the world experience similar struggles. In a podcast that shares the stories about the difficulties that international students face during the COVID-19 pandemic, a student from Jamaica talks about how they are "unable to gain unemployment, with no revenue, and they still have bills to pay for rent and groceries." Being an international student in general, and especially during a pandemic excludes these students from being able to receive support through the federal government. Speaking to my close friends about their situation, opened my eyes to see how many of them really do not feel like they can do anything to solve these challenges. It becomes a matter of succumbing to the system or sinking because of the system.

After receiving the dreaded "Your account is on financial hold" email from the Financial Aid office, I shakenly walked to the office to enquire about what exactly this meant. Walking up to the booth once they called my name, I was met with a hostile attitude, one that made me feel more hopeless about my situation. I remembered feeling a lump in my throat as I asked what my options were, explaining that I was an international student. The woman at the desk looked at me and recited the generic "We can only take you off financial hold, once you have paid the amount in full." I felt like she looked right through me. My status meant nothing to her but everything to the system. It is a hopeless situation to be in, to need a large amount of money, mainly being able to get that through scholarships or loans but being blocked from both opportunities because of your status. Not being able to apply for federal scholarship or any type of loans, left me having to set aside time from schoolwork and focus on finding other ways of getting money. Making sure I am eligible to take classes the next term became my main priority outside of getting good grades. Getting a job on campus was also a hopeless pursuit because those that are citizens and residents are prioritized first. What I also did not realize during the time was that as an international student, you cannot be a full-time student and full-time intern at the same time. My initial hopes of working to that extent and studying at the same time went down the drain.

I started to become increasingly frustrated with a world that seemed to be against me. I felt like a victim because I was put in this endless cycle that was never going to favor me because of my status. Toil after toil, I was running after opportunities and continuously disappointed when the opportunity slipped out of my fingers because of my status.

There was no winning for someone like me when the system was designed to keep me out.

The storm soon calmed, when a few years later, my family and I had the privilege of becoming permanent residents. I realized that my mindset also had to shift because as an international student there are so many realities you face with things that you cannot do, that you just get used to it. I started having a victim mentality, convincing myself that there was no way I can get a scholarship because I am an international student, whereas the reality was that in my second year, I was able to get a scholarship *because* I was an international student. When I became a permanent resident, I also had to switch my mindset because I was now eligible for a lot more opportunities. I had to recognize and stop myself from getting too comfortable with being a victim, because if I carried on that way, even when I had more privileges, I would have still been confined by my victim mentality. With the new revelation that I have access to more scholarships, loans, and general opportunities, I knew I had to take full advantage.

# THE PRINCIPLE OF PERSPECTIVE IS BEST PRACTICED BY CHALLENGING ASSUMPTIONS AND QUESTIONING STANDARDS.

Having international student friends, at some point, I started to feel bad and even guilty that I am almost doing 'too' much when there is so little that they can do. It was like, as international students, we were all in prison but after a while I was released on bail. The guilt and anxiety would creep up in every opportunity I received and soon turned into imposter syndrome, the feeling of being a fraud. I believe with the perspective shift that I had, even if I were still an international student at this point, I would have found a way to take advantage of my status, regardless of whether it affords me more opportunity or less. I think that even getting all these opportunities was just a matter of me putting myself out there, but also knowing that I can leverage my experiences being an international student to get a scholarship or a job opportunity. It is difficult to not allow your mind to become a hindrance to the things you can accomplish in life, but I genuinely believe that the power comes from realizing that you can use your holistic story to obtain different opportunities. It is the principle of perspective and effective storytelling that breaks ground and blazes the trail for others.

Coming to America, as an outsider, enabled me to see things from a fresh perspective. The resources were there, but at least in my first year, I did not take advantage of the resources because I just did not know how to be resourceful. Coming to university forced me to be resourceful because of the lack of resources that were available to me because of my status. It pushed me to go deeper, challenge and question things, which encouraged me to look beyond the default of what I can only see is available to me. In a way, becoming a permanent resident after a few years was not my breakthrough. It had to be more than just my status that had to change. I could have become a permanent resident, but still not taken advantage of opportunities.

It relates closely to how my friends, family and I handled the effects of COVID-19 in the initial stages. I used to claim that I would be more productive and achieve more if I just had more time. The pandemic swept through the country and gave me the opportunity to have more time. What we see in both cases is that even amid opportunity, your perspective decides whether to walk towards or away from it. I used to use the "if only" excuse as a crutch, so much so that even when my 'desire' was realized, I was paralyzed because my environment changed, but my mindset did not.

# RECEIVE AND REFLECT - LEADERSHIP

**My thoughts:**
The common misbelief surrounding leadership is that it solely accompanies seniority or a paid position. I've reshaped my understanding of leadership—it's not confined to titles but encompasses actions and behaviors that inspire people toward a shared goal or greater good. Don't delay taking on a leadership role until it's officially bestowed upon you or tied to a job title. Leadership isn't exclusive to the workplace; it can manifest in any situation. Regardless of your current circumstances, you have the capacity to lead by seizing the initiative. Often, the most transformative leaders are those who recognize that leadership isn't about authority; it's about influence and the ability to spark positive change. So, don't underestimate the power you hold to lead in your daily interactions, be it within a team project, a community initiative, or even a casual conversation.

---

**Self-reflection questions:**

- In my view, what does success truly mean?

- What qualities of an effective leader do I currently possess?

- Can I find chances to mentor or guide others, even if I don't hold a conventional leadership position?

---

# SURVIVOR VS. STEWARD

The chapter "Survivor vs. Steward" explores the concept of personal responsibility in relation to the environment and resources. It delves into the differences between being a mere survivor, who uses resources without regard to their impact, and being a steward, who actively cares for their environment and manages resources sustainably.

# 6 SURVIVOR VS. STEWARD

I would never have thought that I would experience being brought down by other women, rather than being pulled up by them. What do you do when the water that is supposed to keep your boat afloat drowns you instead? It's a helpless and hopeless feeling. Confused and drifting into the unknown, I fought between the state of survival and stewardship. To survive is to float, tread the water, and breathe. To steward is to acknowledge the fact that one is floating, leverage it, and start swimming. The fine line between being a survivor and a steward was whether I chose to use what was pushing me down, to pull me up. Once again, the choice was mine.

Being in the College of Computing and Informatics at Drexel University, I saw many of the women that were Computer Science students, change their majors to something less technical or completely different. My friends and I, who started as Computer Science students and later switched, realized that this was a problem that was much bigger than our personal situations. We weren't alone in this struggle. Many women had entered the realm of Computer Science, but very few remained in it. It became clear that this problem extended far beyond our individual experiences.

In the summer of 2017, a mission was born. We needed to uncover the root causes of this issue. Was it a lack of support for women in the field, the way courses were taught, or something else entirely? We embarked on a journey to find answers, sharing our experiences on social media. The response was overwhelming, and it became evident that we were not alone in our concerns.

Buoyed by the positive feedback, I decided to take things a

step further. I reached out to female faculty members at Drexel's College of Computing and Informatics, eager for their support, advice, and the opportunity to speak with women who had experienced what I was going through.

One faculty member said,

"This sounds like a great idea for a project, and I would be happy to help in any way that I can. There is a lot of interest in supporting women in computing and informatics and strengthening our numbers at Drexel."

Another echoed,

"Congrats on taking the initiative to start such an effort."

But the most unexpected response came when the Dean's secretary reached out to invite me for a meeting with the Dean himself.

In that moment, I realized that I was being summoned to use my voice and actions to effect change within my university. As I sat before the Dean of my College, I proposed an idea, one that he greeted with unwavering support and encouragement. It was from that point on that I, along with a faculty member and two co-founders, would spend the summer of 2017 creating a program aimed at addressing these pressing issues.

By September 2017, I was appointed as the Chair of Retention for the student organization 'Women in Computing Society' (WiCS), and our initiative officially became a program under WiCS. The Freshwoman Cohort Program (FCP) was born, designed to encourage and retain 40 female students in the College of Computing and Informatics. We recognized that the first year was a critical period in which students explored and made vital decisions about their future. Our mission was to ensure that female students entering the Computer Science program did not change majors due to a lack of support or representation.

For a time, it seemed that our efforts were having the desired impact. But success came with its own set of challenges. My co-founders and I were accused of being 'too' active on campus, and our program was intentionally structured under the official student organization, to avoid conflict due to fear of competition. The suggestion which first came from a place of providing infrastructural support, soon started to crumble that very system. Despite our best intentions, we faced backlash from unexpected sources. One such source was the faculty advisor for my program, who also advised the official student organization. Her attitude shifted as she saw our program gaining more recognition than the one, she officially advised. She began to speak poorly of us to a female executive board of the official organization and other faculty members. But the most shocking blow came when I discovered that an executive board member of the official organization had spoken negatively about me to a potential internship employer with whom I was about to interview. As I entered the interview, it was clear that the employer had already formed a negative opinion of me. In those moments, it was difficult not to question my actions and behaviors. I wondered if I had gone "too far,", if I was doing too much.

## When Doubt Turned to Confidence

As doubt began to creep in, I questioned whether my actions were too bold, whether I was being too active on the platform. My prior experiences with the conflict surrounding the retention program left me wondering if these questions and statements were detrimental. I grappled with imposter syndrome, a feeling of being a fraud. I remembered the quiet person I had been in high school, and I contemplated retreating to my comfort zone.

But then, something shifted.

Don't waste the rain, they say. And in my life, the rain came in the form of Angela. A pivotal encounter with Angela, (a Drexel alumni and my scholarship donor) would prove to be the lifeline I so desperately needed. She believed in me when others seemed to doubt me. Angela was not just a scholarship donor; she became a mentor and friend who believed in my mission and saw the impact we were making on campus. She reminded me that the strength I had shown in my journey was an inspiration to others. Angela's unwavering support rekindled my determination and helped me regain my focus. As I contemplated her words, I came to a profound realization - being active on campus wasn't the problem. The real issue was when one's actions were perceived as a threat to others. There was a silent pressure to conform, to blend in, to go unnoticed. But I resolved to use that pressure as a catalyst, to break free from those constraints, and to remain unapologetic about my mission.

With each step I took, more opportunities revealed themselves. During this period, I interned at a startup, my very first work experience. It was there that I delved deeper into the world of LinkedIn and recognized the power this platform held. I used it to share more of my journey as a woman in Computing, to tell my personal story to anyone who would listen. This expanded my reach, and my content began to populate the feeds of peers and fellow students on campus. People began to recognize me as "Blessing from LinkedIn," and I heard comments like, "Why do I keep seeing your name and content on my LinkedIn?" I couldn't help but question if these statements were genuine compliments or simply expressions of annoyance. The battle with self-doubt raged on, however, the scarcity of student presence on LinkedIn meant that my seemingly ordinary efforts appeared extraordinary to others. As I navigated this challenging period, my guiding principle remained clear. As the years went on, Drexel's College of Computing and Informatics became the breeding ground that birthed "Boundless Blessing" – a woman that would be bold enough to take a seat, yet humble enough to leave a seat.

## My encouragement to you

You are not weak, a failure, or inadequate if you're still trying to figure out how to tread the waters of life. Your journey, just like mine, is unique. Every step, every obstacle, every challenge has brought you to where you are today.

Regardless of whether you've faced a season of highs or lows, remember that every step is a part of your journey. Each obstacle, each accomplishment is a part of your story. Don't define your identity by a single season; instead, learn to steward each moment well. As the days turned into weeks, and the weeks into months, I recognized that even in my moments of doubt, I had come further than I ever imagined. The journey of self-discovery and self-realization continued, and the lessons I learned were invaluable.

Whether you're floating, treading water, or swimming, know that you are bound to be boundless. The challenges you face today are the steppingstones to your future. You have the strength, resilience, and the potential to move forward.

If you've faced a season of highs: I want to celebrate you for overcoming the obstacles that led you to the top of the mountain. I want to encourage you to lift as you climb. I want to warn you not to define your identity by this season, but instead learn to steward each peak well. Familiarity breeds contempt.

If you've faced a season of lows: I want to commend you for your fight and efforts. Especially the battles that are only seen behind the scenes. I want to remind you that you are not alone. Try again. You are still worthy of a fresh start. Wherever you are in this season of life, remember that every challenge, every trial, and every obstacle is an opportunity to grow. You've made it this far, and you're capable of achieving even more. Keep treading, keep swimming.

## Letting go of baggage

Navigating new relationships with the weight of past trauma and unhealed wounds is akin to walking on a tightrope suspended high above a gap. The story of my journey through the waves of past hurts and my quest for healing began in the virtual office of my therapist. I'll never forget the day she introduced me to the term "gaslighting." It's a form of psychological and emotional abuse, cunning in its subtlety. It preys on the vulnerabilities of the heart, often leaving the victim emotionally scarred. The scars I bore, not only from the emotional manipulation but also from the physical abuse endured in a past relationship, ran deep.

Gaslighting's insidious grasp had me perpetually doubting myself. I felt too sensitive, quick to apologize even when I knew I was not at fault. Blame was my constant companion, and I carried it willingly. In the world of healing and growth, the choice between being a survivor and a steward is a pivotal crossroads. As I embarked on my journey of transformation, I faced the daunting task of reconciling my past traumas with the potential of a future filled with love and self-discovery.

The survivor in me carried the weight of my scars, believing that every relationship was bound to replay the horrors of my past. I had been hurt, abused, and left emotionally battered. To me, love was a minefield, and every gesture was a potential trigger. This survivor mentality had me bracing for the worst, unable to truly embrace a new relationship. The pain of my history still cast a long shadow over my heart. Yet, within the wave of my healing, I discovered the power of becoming a steward. It wasn't about denying the past; it was about transforming it into wisdom and strength. Stewardship was the beacon of hope and resilience, the path that led me to recovery. In my quest to become a steward of my own heart, I turned to faith and divine grace. It was through my renewed connection with God that I began to comprehend the difference between being a survivor of my past and a steward of my future. It was here that I found the courage to face the demons of my past without letting them define my future. Understanding the transition from past pain to a hopeful future is like deciphering a complex riddle. It's about recognizing the fine line between past traumas affecting the present and the essence of your partner's character. Misunderstanding this line can trigger panic, compelling one to flee from relationships. It poses questions: When is the right time to step into a new relationship, and when should the focus remain on healing?

Love becomes a puzzle. The past distorts its meaning. "I love you" is tinged with pain, associated with a slap or emotional cruelty. I too, once uttered those words through tears and bruises. How does one, who's familiar with love in its most perverted form, come to understand its purest essence? Each day, I learn that healing is a process. It's about recognizing when the time is right, when you've reached the precipice of your past, and the fear of it no longer blinds you. It's about realizing that love should be kind, patient, and not something to be endured but embraced. And through it all, I'm on a path to discovering love in its purest form, one scar at a time.

# RECEIVE AND REFLECT- RESOURCEFULNESS

**My thoughts:**
It is no surprise that life comes with its fair share of financial, academic, spiritual, physical, emotional, and mental challenges. These challenges force us into thinking that we do not have what we need to overcome those challenges. What we find is that the problem is not related to the lack of resources, but the inability to be resourceful. By challenging assumptions and questioning things, we open ourselves to see our problems from a renewed perspective. We start to see things from a place of advantage rather than disadvantage. An opportunity rather than an obstacle. Sometimes we have to create the solution that we want to see.

**Self-reflection questions:**
• Who has encountered a similar challenge, and what strategies did they employ to overcome it?

• If a solution isn't readily available, can I, or someone within my network, generate a viable solution?

• What resources am I lacking and how can I use what I have to bridge the gap?

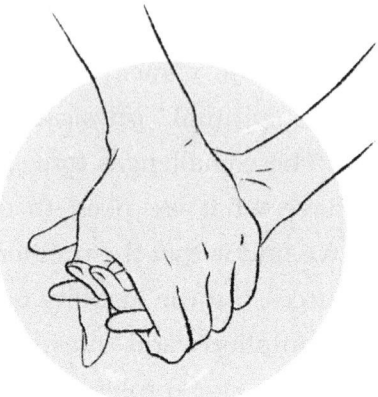

# THE PURPOSE AND POWER OF PEOPLE

"Purpose and Power of People" explores the significance of individuals
and their role in shaping the world. It delves into the idea that each
person has a unique purpose and the potential to make a lasting impact
on society. There is an extreme importance and responsibility of
harnessing one's personal power and using it for the betterment of
others and the world.

# 7 THE PURPOSE AND POWER OF PEOPLE

Have you ever caught yourself observing people? Forming narratives of the stories they could have? Trying to trace the paths they have traveled? During the summer of 2019, my 2-hour commute to New York City led me to a wealth of stories. Walking into a hot, cramped, New York City subway was like walking into a rundown library. Internally filled to the brim with stories, externally in a state of neglect.

Standing in the subway on the way to my summer internship, I saw many things. I narrated many stories in my head. I formed conclusions that I had no right in making. At first, it was just to pass time. Then it was out of sheer curiosity. Every person that I saw had a purpose. I do not just mean the people that looked put together on the outside. Every person: the young mother pleading for her son to just sit down, the homeless veteran asking for change, the man in a suit frantically trying to reschedule a meeting, the group of school kids being school kids. I saw people being looked down on, stepped over and avoided for the way they looked and behaved. I saw different types of people and how they were treated. It would be a lie to say that the reactions of others did not taint my perspective and the way I thought about the stories of each of them. That was the problem.

Take away the office, the ragged clothes, the title, the sleeping bag, and you are left with a human. The layers of privilege are just a bonus. When we train ourselves to see past the privilege, we get to gain a deeper understanding of a person. The most eye-opening insight I drew from this was that despite outward appearance and background, everyone was riding the same subway. Everyone that was riding the subway had a purpose. Little did I know that this was a reminder that I would need to cling onto later in life. My commute became one of the most edifying experiences that summer. It was not just about treating everyone with the same level of respect but seeing everyone as a human first. My world was transformed when I saw people not with my eyes, but with my heart.

## The Power of People

It was not always this way. I used to think that my purpose in life was to be used and emotionally abused by others. My self-esteem was at rock bottom. It was a conclusion that I thought I had to live by, because that had been the life I had lived. I did not trust people easily because I had been bitten too many times. Too many people had bullied me, laughed at me, used me, and left me. The rejection I had received from others, soon turned into self-reflection. My life became a story of "Blessing against the world". As I built the strongest wall between myself and everyone else, I became powerless. I abused the power of people, by giving people too much power over me. It is interesting how people tend to surround themselves with broken people, when they too are broken. It does not heal, it harms. It took years for me to chip away at this wall, but I learned to see the journey as the destination and the process as the goal.

The journey revealed the impact I can have on others and the things I can do, once I embrace who I am and use what I have. My problem was that the longer I waited, the more the weight of my excuses crushed my potential opportunities and prospective relationships.

## The Purpose of People

By carrying too many people's burdens, I started to get crushed under the pressure of trying to please everyone.

The realization that I couldn't bear the burdens of the world on my shoulders came as a profound awakening. For far too long, I had attempted to carry the weight of everyone's problems, believing that it was my duty to please and support everyone around me. It was as though I had convinced myself that I could be the savior for all, even while I was still navigating the journey of self-discovery.

Perhaps, in retrospect, it was a way to avoid confronting my own personal challenges. By immersing myself in the needs of others, I could sidestep the complexities of my own life. It was a path that led to self-neglect and the gradual erosion of my own well-being. It was a heavy load to bear, and I was learning the hard way that it was unsustainable.

The turning point came when I realized that I needed to let go of this unnecessary burden. I needed to free myself from the expectation of being everything to everybody. The weight I had been carrying was never meant for a single pair of shoulders. It was then that I began to reorient my life towards a more purpose-driven path, starting from within and radiating outward, from the depths of my heart.

This new perspective on burdens was transformative. I understood that burdens were meant to be shared, not shouldered alone or passed from one person to another. It was a revelation that allowed me to open up to people in a different way, listening to their stories without feeling the overwhelming need to save them. I recognized that the true power of connection lies in the ability to empathize and grow together, not in shouldering one another's loads.

It dawned on me that by welcoming new people into my life, I was inviting new perspectives, new thinking, and new dimensions of growth. Those walls I thought were remnants of isolation turned out to be bridges, connecting me to individuals whose stories and experiences enriched my own. I realized that life wasn't meant to be a solitary journey; true thriving required a community.

For me, it took a village to help me see the light. This village of family, friends, mentors, and kindred spirits played a pivotal role in my transformation. Their unwavering support and guidance bolstered me, helping me shed the weight of false expectations. Together, we built bridges of understanding and empathy, and in that collective journey, I discovered the immense strength of community.

## A Person of Purpose and Power

There was a time when I spent a Saturday morning talking to prospective students at Drexel University about my untraditional experience as a student. As I was sitting on the stage, looking out to the hundreds of students, I could only wish I were sitting in their seats in my senior year of high school. I wished that someone would have poured into me and given me a glimpse of guidance, assurance, and hope. I did not have that. It was a tough lesson to learn, but I had to convince myself that one can use what was absent in their life to create a positive presence in someone else's. I truly believe that it was someone's obedience to this, that brought me to where I am. I am learning that even in obscurity, there is opportunity. Even in absence, there is presence. Even in darkness, there is light. I was not created to sit around and wait for eternity. I am called to engage in the world, to create culture and to be productive in serving the needs of those around me through my life and work. My purpose is connected to people. I cannot run away from it.

It does not take a 'perfect' story to impact people, it just takes 'a' story. It took sharing my story to realize a leader is not a leader because they know more, but because they do what is best for the people that are following them. That day, I led prospective students to open the door of hope, potential and possibility. In the same way, no matter what your experience has been with people, good or bad, I hope that this reminder encourages you that you are a person of power, called for a purpose, to serve people.

As the daughter of a professor, my life was marked by the ebb and flow of academic communities. With each passing academic year, familiar faces departed, making way for new arrivals. Amid the shifting academic landscapes, I learned the invaluable role of shared experiences and collective support. It was in these academic communities that I truly comprehended the power of collaboration, empathy, and the deep connections we establish with others. I discovered that community isn't a static concept but a dynamic, living force that profoundly influences us, sustains us, and reminds us of our deep interconnectedness. It's within these communities that we unearth the strength to share our stories, effect positive change, and ignite hope for those who follow in our footsteps.

Every year, for as long as I can remember, our Christmas parties took on a unique and heartwarming character. It was a tradition that infused warmth, goodwill, and the spirit of togetherness. Our home became a sanctuary for international students who couldn't make it back to their own homes during the holiday season. These students, often far from their families, created an eclectic and vibrant tapestry of cultures, languages, and traditions that interwove with our own festive celebrations. Christmas at our place wasn't just about sharing the joy of the season; it was about embracing the diversity and unity that comes with it. The house resonated with laughter and conversation in various languages, the exchange of stories and customs, and the delightful aroma of dishes from every corner of the globe.

## Dealing with Diversity of People

In the world of relationships, we're all like pages from different books, each one bearing the marks of our individual stories. I'm 25 years old, and in my journey through life, I've realized that it's our unique experiences that make us who we are. One thing that's struck me is how different life experiences can play a significant role in our relationships. You see, I've had moments when my voice felt small, like a whisper in a storm. Times when it seemed like nobody was listening, and my thoughts were disregarded, pulling me back into the shadows of self-doubt. What's fascinating, and sometimes challenging, is how these experiences can affect our interactions with others. For instance, there are those who are naturally outgoing, wearing their words like vibrant garments, or individuals who assert themselves with unwavering confidence. These interactions can sometimes trigger old insecurities, requiring understanding of one's stories and compromising solutions. Then there are the stories of diverse upbringings. I've been lucky to call many places home, each one contributing unique perspectives and challenges to my life canvas. But when I meet someone who has lived their entire life in one place, it's like two artists trying to blend different shades of paint.

Our experiences, whether joyful or painful, shape our thoughts and actions. As we venture into relationships, it becomes clear that these experiences are an integral part of who we are. It's essential to honor these differences and approach them with empathy. Sometimes, assumptions can lead to misunderstandings, and it's always better to have an open dialogue.

## Voices and Choices

People use their voices every day. To elevate and deflate. There are days where I would speak words of encouragement, love, and upliftment to myself. There are days where I purposely put myself down, convincing myself that I am something that I am not. The voices we hear and are surrounded by every hour, every month, and every year, impact, and shape not only the way we see ourselves, but the way we see our future. When I took a step back to connect the voices I have heard and my life circumstances, I found that the value that I placed on certain words and messages—influenced the way I lived. The positive voices brought me into the light and the negative voices dragged me deeper into the dark. It was the noise that confused me more than anything. I struggled to tell the difference between positive and negative. I started to listen to everything, but still placed more value on the negative. Looking back, I see that the choice was nothing but mine. I chose to listen to the negative voices. What surprised me is how little value I placed on the positive voices, maybe because they came from close friends and family. Familiarity breeds contempt. I had heard the encouragement of those close to me, too many times that I became desensitized to the positive voices. What if I had listened to those positive voices more? Where would I be now? The voices are still there. It is noisier than ever, but the choice is still mine and the choice is now.

Any time that inner voice tries to tell you who you cannot be, you need to remember who you are. We all have it. What choice will you make? What voice will you give value to?

## When "Is this it?" turns to "This is it!"

Navigating the readiness for any meaningful connection, whether it's in the context of friendships or romantic relationships, can be a complex journey. It often involves understanding the distinction between recognizing your current capacity for such connections and the idea of waiting until you feel "perfect" for them. It's a fine balance that I've been grappling with for the past few years.

A significant moment occurred when I had the opportunity to listen to a talk by someone who shared profound insights about human connections. He emphasized the critical importance of having certain fundamentals and a strong foundation before entering any kind of connection. Without these essentials, even the most promising connections can crumble, whether it's immediately evident or becomes apparent over time. The concept of readiness is not always straightforward. We've all heard narratives in movies and TV shows about "the right person at the wrong time" or "the wrong person at the right time." It raises questions about those instances when it's the right person at the right time.

While such cases might be rare, waiting is not inherently wrong.

Our culture has subtly ingrained impatience in us. Phrases like "Carpe Diem!" and societal pressures about age and connections can make us feel like waiting is a mistake. We tend to rush things and get frustrated when we're asked to wait, like being put in the friend zone. But I wonder, what would happen if the impatient one did pursue a connection with the person who needed more time? How many conflicts, misunderstandings, and fights would arise before they found stability? Is it truly worth the rush?

Impatience is a natural emotion, but we should also ask where it comes from. Can we put aside our longing for the sake of healthy growth? And why the rush? Have we taken the time to prepare ourselves? I'm reminded that perhaps there is a rhythm to life that we must acknowledge. The narrative of 'seizing the moment' often overshadows the importance of nurturing and allowing growth to occur naturally. The concept of readiness should be embraced in its full complexity. It is not about achieving perfection but about building a strong foundation within us.

# IT'S NOT ABOUT WAITING FOR THE PERFECT MOMENT, BUT ABOUT BEING PREPARED TO EMBRACE THE MUSIC OF CONNECTION WHEN IT PLAYS ITS SWEETEST TUNE.

## Finding My Voice

In my journey, I've often wondered about my struggle with speaking up. It's not as severe as it may sound, but lately, I've found myself unable to find my voice in both professional and personal settings. I'm still on a quest to understand the roots of this challenge.

In professional settings, the struggle often surfaces when I'm put on the spot or faced with a question I'm not immediately prepared to answer. It's as if I momentarily lose my ability to speak, and I catch myself behaving in ways that I'd love to observe from an outsider's perspective. Of course, there are techniques and strategies to overcome this, to find my voice, but I've come to believe that it's even wiser to prevent the triggers that cause this silence.

A similar challenge emerges in my personal life, especially during conversations with friends. Depending on the situation, I often find myself silently listening rather than interjecting. There are moments when even this silence becomes a trigger. In those situations, it should be straightforward to say something like, 'Let me pause you for a moment' to correct any misconceptions or 'I'd prefer not to receive advice right now.' But, for the sake of courtesy, I sometimes feel anchored in my chair, unable to speak up.

This challenge is relative, but my desire is clear – I want to learn how to express myself when something doesn't sit right with me. Additionally, I aim to cultivate the habit of asking questions like 'Do you want me to simply listen, or are you open to advice?' after someone shares their thoughts. I believe such questions are valuable because assumptions based on our own understanding often lead to miscommunication, a lack of support, and misunderstandings. They serve as a safeguard, steering away from the 'wrong actions' and preventing the recipient from nurturing 'blind expectations.'

Certainly, asking these questions won't guarantee a perfect conversation, but it's a step in the right direction. Simple inquiries can offer the clarity needed to provide the best support possible. Similarly, when I'm on the receiving end, I also aim to articulate my preferences. Whether it's stating, 'I'm looking for a listening ear right now, not advice' or 'I think this conversation has gone on long enough, and I need a break from it.' Effective communication is crucial. It's not about expecting Person A to read your mind and respond accordingly, it's about being open about your needs and reciprocally asking about theirs. This doesn't make anyone weak in communication. It's about nurturing mutual understanding, recognizing that everyone communicates differently, and acknowledging that we have unique lessons to teach and learn within each relationship.

Delving into the roots of these challenges, I believe they trace back to feelings of inadequacy, stemming from a cycle of encounters with toxic individuals. I've experienced being misunderstood, and at times, I've held the unusual, slowly fading belief that I'm here solely to be used. This led to hesitance in speaking up for myself – thoughts like, 'How dare I?' permeated my mind. It's not always about accommodating others at my own expense. Sometimes, the thought of evolving into a different person can be intimidating. Would I risk losing friendships over it? Would I question the quality of those friendships, wondering if they would prefer the quiet me over the assertive me because it's more convenient and comfortable for them?

I understand that this journey requires unlearning and replanting. But it's one that should be the norm, even though I've made the abnormal my everyday life. Unlearning, recognizing the roots, and cultivating a healthier and more assertive self is a path I'm eager to explore.

# RECEIVE AND REFLECT - RELATIONSHIPS

**My thoughts:**

As I've gone through life, I've seen how having or not having relationships can mess with how I see and value people. There was this phase when I thought I could do without friendships or relationships, like it was me against the world. The idea of getting close to someone freaked me out – the thought that I could get ditched, let down, or just shoved aside. But as the years rolled on, I figured out how crucial relationships are for my own growth. Some folks think being picky about who you hang with and being intentional about relationships are the same thing. But I've learned it's not just about being picky; it's about being careful with who you let into your life and putting effort into the relationships you decide to keep. Those connections really shape who you are. We're not built to go through this life all alone. No matter how many times you've been let down or left behind, there are people out there who'll lift you up and make sure you know you're seen and loved.

---

**Self-reflection questions:**

- What are my love languages (to give and receive)?

- Which negative trait do I aim to release from my life?

- Who have I given excessive influence and access to in my life?

---

# EMPTY YOUR CUP

In the practice of martial arts, it is said that before learning, one must first "empty their cup." In order to truly absorb and understand new knowledge, one must let go of preconceived notions and biases, and approach learning with an open mind. This concept applies not only to martial arts, but also to other areas of our lives. By learning to empty our cup, we open ourselves up to new possibilities and experiences, and ultimately become boundless in our growth and understanding.

# 8 EMPTY YOUR CUP

Driving home that weekend was the greatest conviction I had ever felt. It made me cry and weep from my stomach. It was a deep hurt that could not be contained. How could such an amazing weekend have turned into such a sad time in my life? I had travelled to Maryland to spend time with some of my friends. We relished each other's company as we enjoyed a delightful meal, engaged in games and shared our stories. The atmosphere was filled with warmth and love, until suddenly a mighty wind swept me into the desert of my mind. At a point during these activities, I felt triggered by the obvious reality that I could not relate to conversations about their experiences in Nigeria. I would find myself staring into the distance as they chatted away. It was like I was standing in this dry, barren land. This new, yet so familiar environment made me feel parched. I could not speak, so I resorted to feigned laughter and feigned interest. It was a trigger that gave me a deep sense of loneliness as I was reminded that I don't belong anywhere. Or at least so I thought. I sank into the couch, sulking at the fact that, despite legalities, I wasn't Nigerian *enough* to add to the conversation. Or how it was translated in my mind, I just wasn't enough.

It dawned on me how 'unrelatable' I was. A figure of speech exists that goes "Jack of all trades, master of none" which relates to the idea that someone can do many things but is not an expert in one. Depending on who you talk to, this can be an insult. I see a reflection of this in my own life though, relating to my childhood, or lack thereof. For me, home became everywhere and nowhere. I was constantly in transition – a rootless nomad on a restless journey. I feared that the inability to make friends or relate to them was due to the instability of my upbringing. When you feel empty in a world that is empty, you have nowhere to go but to reside in the deepest, darkest thoughts of your mind.

When you are surrounded by people, yet still feel lonely, your heart aches at the fact that being misunderstood may just be the only constant you face. Each experience, school, friendship, memory that I had to leave behind, took a piece of my heart with it. Ignoring these problems only stored up trouble. My cup was full, but with filthy water.

## Empty your cup

Everyone is wired with a desire to feel connected or to feel some form of belonging. I was yearning to be understood by friends who could never fully understand me. I imagine myself standing 5 centimeters away from a 6-foot painting. The meaning of the painting can easily be misunderstood if you are standing too close. Standing there, craving to find a meaning for the painting came to no avail, because I didn't see the bigger picture—I couldn't. If you can't understand the bigger picture, you will not know how you fit in. Sometimes it's our close proximity to a problem that causes us the most pain. The closer I got, the more my vision became blurred. I came to the realization that my pain wasn't primarily connected to my friends; rather, it stemmed from the identity crisis that had been a constant in my life. Only my family could understand what I went through because they had gone through it themselves. It's unfortunate because sometimes our thirst for answers can consume us so much that we forget to step back and ask a different question. Was it the presence or lack of something that made me feel this way? Was it the experience with my friends that made me feel empty or was it me feeling detached from my family? This emotional numbness I felt came from within (the house), and it affected every aspect of my life.

When we empty our cups, we can unlearn self-imposed limitations, and fill ourselves up with something new. On my 3-hour journey back home from my weekend trip to Maryland, I felt this huge burden that drove me to tears. I just had to let it all out. This realization brought to light the absence of a genuine connection with my family. All the thoughts, questions, and emotions I had been concealing were becoming too much to bear. The profound loneliness was devouring me, and with each passing moment, I felt myself shrinking. I needed to scream, so I did. For the entire 3-hour journey home, within the comfort of my car, I let out everything that I had stored over the years. The dam finally burst. I realized that though I had been able to steward my academics, career, and personal brand well, my family life was severely lacking. It was the greatest conviction I had ever felt because I left it too long.

Once I arrived home, I sat my family down and initiated one of our most candid conversations ever. Gradually, the emotional void that I had been longing to fill for years, was filled through the restoration of my family relationship. As we opened up about our personal journeys of being global nomads, I felt like I was finally part of the conversation. Our journeys themselves became home. As I listened to the experiences of my mother, father, sister and brother, I understood that my home was right here all along. It was never about the place, but the people. I guess you could say that I inadvertently hardened my heart against them after every move. It wasn't their fault; they were just the collateral damage of the stormy sea I was facing. Our conversations felt like I was coming up for the freshest breath of air. It was refreshing, invigorating and eased my fear of the unknown. I finally saw the bigger picture. Home.

OUR JOURNEYS THEMSELVES BECAME HOME.

**You are enough**

I used to feel like my upbringing and the past places where I lived were like really old photographs that start to crumble when I hold them in my hand. As soon as I felt like I had a good grip, it disappeared. Every move triggered anxiety and stress. Though I felt like I was a citizen of nowhere on Earth, I came to know that I am a citizen of Heaven. That night of conviction and revelation, I was given a new identity. Not a crisis, but in Christ. That is what really mattered, that identity. I realized that what I needed, I already had. Sometimes it is just as simple as that. All you have is all you need (at the time). As I grew deeper relationships with my family members and learned to steward the present, I was reminded how when God is going to fill something, it must be empty first. Prior to this, I convinced myself that I was never enough. Though it was not me, but the people and places where I was looking for approval from. They could never be enough. My faith has taught me that the emptiest places in my heart can only be filled by God. The deepest thirst of my soul can only be quenched by God. He is able to fill the emptiness with living water, in which I will never thirst again. I can drink the cup of suffering and still remain victorious. That's the beauty of it.

This new understanding allowed me to re-learn how to build deeper friendships and relationships. Not from a place of offense but understanding. After blaming relationships and avoiding friendships for triggering my emptiness, I had to reconcile with those who I had pushed away. Standing firm in the knowledge that I am enough; I was able to pour more into my friendships. Rather than tainting my friendships with the filthy waters I had accumulated, I discovered emotional freedom in the depths of purer, living water. Know that, even as you expect transparency and anticipate deliverance, you will experience some turbulence, but you will surely arrive at your destination. Amidst your journey, be mindful not to overlook the transformations occurring within you. One of my favorite writers, Morgan Harper Nichols, wrote a piece that captured my learnings beautifully,

"Even in the seasons where you feel empty and restrained by a lack of opportunity, there is still a well of possibility stirring within you.

You are filled to the brim with stories and experiences that have helped you grow in wisdom. You are a survivor of the stormiest seas that gave you a beautiful strength well beyond your years."[iv]

So, as a survivor of one of the stormiest seas, I'm asking you: what have you been storing for too long? What cup do you finally need to empty? What limitations do you need to break free from? Don't wait until it's too late. This is your reminder to empty your cup and withstand the pain of emptiness because the filling is coming soon.

## Default vs. Destined Life

EVERY DEFAULT PATH WAS A DESTINED PATH THAT SOMEONE HAD TO DISCOVER.

I could never appreciate the destined life if I had never walked the default path. It served its purpose. Growing up, I was living life through trial and error. Figuring out life for yourself is not a bad thing, but following society's blueprint can be a dangerous plan to follow. I had tried so many different things to figure out my identity and to find the answers to the burning questions I had about my upbringing. Turning to the world for my answers almost led to my detriment. Throughout the course of my life, I had been walking in the dark, holding on to any rope that I could find, hoping that it would lead me onto the right path. The rope led me to get involved with the 'wrong' crowds at school, it led me to make future decisions based on what others might think, it led me to believe that my identity is singular.

Funding a scholarship was another default path that I had convinced myself I would only be able to accomplish once I had reached a certain place in life: whether that refers to my status or my brand, company, or the amount of money I have. It did not even cross my mind that a student can create a scholarship for other students in university. As a student who also needed financial assistance, it did not seem like the wisest mission to embark on. I have been firsthand witness to how the foolish things of the world are used to humble the wise. As the post about my scholarship idea circulated through my network, I received messages from both students and professionals who were in awe of what I was able to pull off. I gained a sense of accomplishment, a new sense of confidence when it comes to setting ambitious goals and reaching them. This opportunity to give to others was like someone handing me a lamp whilst walking in the dark, which illuminated the destined path in front of me.

With discernment, I realized that I did not have the monetary resources, but I did have the human resources around me that I could leverage (a network of over 13,000 people that I had built at that point). The principle of perspective taught me that I did not need to wait to have everything that I needed. I did not wait to have the status, the money, or the other boxes that I felt needed to be ticked to fund a scholarship. By focusing on what I did have, a network and community that I had built over two years, I was able to crowdfund over $2,500 to support the education of 5 international students across the United States. This was not only for the sake of giving international students money. It was a way of showing people and therefore living out what it means to live a destined life.

Despite lacking the personal funds to sponsor this scholarship, I successfully crowdfunded it through my extensive network. It was through this self-awareness that I was able to help 5 international students. If I tackled this opportunity with a default mindset, waiting 10, 15 years or until I had it "all together", then these international students might have also missed out on this opportunity. Beyond the monetary aspect of this scholarship, my sincere desire was to assist people in mindset shift, persuading them that as students, they can achieve significant milestones without waiting for every aspect of life to be perfect. I started to think, if one keeps waiting, how can they be so sure that they will do it when the time comes; most importantly, how can they be so sure that the time will come? Through my actions, I wanted to continue to debunk myths and shatter excuses that a lot of people, including students and professionals have, that stop them from doing something or supporting someone else.

Attending Drexel University as an International Student turned Permanent Resident was a blessing in disguise. In my 5 years as a Drexel student, I had the privilege of obtaining 3 summer internships and 3 co-ops. As part of the Drexel curriculum, I spent my 6-month placements at Frontline Selling, Comcast and Bloomberg. In between those, I spent 3 months interning at Google, Morgan

Stanley, and Microsoft over the summer periods between my second and fourth year. Being a permanent resident afforded me the opportunity to be a full-time student and full-time intern. This was the breakthrough and revelation that helped me pay for university. Taking full advantage of the opportunity, I explored companies in different industries from technology to finance. I like to say that all my internships were secured in a very untraditional way, in the sense that for my 3 summer internships, I did not get them by traditionally applying online the same way a lot of students do. All of them were indirectly obtained through LinkedIn - either through a person that I met on the platform that introduced me to an opportunity, or a community (Rewriting the Code) that I was part of that exposed me to an opportunity.

I chose the destined path because not many people have the privilege of doing so. I promised myself that with every ounce of 'freedom' I have, I will learn to thrive, and not merely survive. I channeled my guilt of 'taking up space' into leveraging the power of storytelling to share my story on LinkedIn. I could not keep quiet about my accomplishments not because I like to boast, but because I know that my playing small does not serve the world. My intention has always been to create room for those that will come after me, so I decided that if I am taking a seat at the table, I will also leave a seat. Breaking out of the default path and into the destined life allowed me to use what was absent in my own life to create a positive presence in the lives of others.

## The Characteristics of Living a Default Life

The characteristics of a default life often resemble a blueprint that society, either consciously or subconsciously, lays out for individuals to follow. This blueprint isn't necessarily negative; it can emerge from the collective experiences of people who have blazed their own trails or from a compilation of articles, blogs, and social media posts offering advice on the paths one should take. Over time, these stories and experiences become the default route or the most common trajectory for many.

The challenge arises when individuals begin to perceive this default path as the only viable option. They may come to believe that this predefined route is the sole means of reaching their desired destination, whether that goal is related to education, a career, or any other aspect of life. The danger lies in the blurring of lines, the rigidity of thought, and the notion that deviation from this established path is an act of rebellion or nonconformity.

In truth, life is far more nuanced and diverse than any single blueprint can encompass. There is no one-size-fits-all approach to success or fulfillment. Each person's journey is a unique narrative, rich with individual experiences, challenges, and victories. It's important to remember that the default path is just one of many possibilities, and while it may provide valuable guidance, it should never confine us to a singular way of thinking.

When we open our minds to the multitude of paths available, we empower ourselves to make choices that align with our true aspirations, values, and goals. It's in the diversity of experiences and the courage to explore uncharted territories that we discover the richness of life.

So, while the default path may be a helpful guide, it should never shackle our potential for growth, exploration, and self-discovery.

## The Characteristics of Living a Destined Life

In contrast, the characteristics of a destined life don't necessarily reject the default path; instead, they reflect the profound understanding that the default path is just one among many possible journeys. A destined life is defined by the knowledge and courage to deconstruct the default path, recognizing that it's a composite of various unique paths woven together. It involves acknowledging that even while treading the default path, the presence of a pivot should not be perceived as the end of the world, but rather as an inspiration to explore alternative routes. It's a mindset driven by curiosity, freedom, and flexibility, one that continually seeks to uncover what lies beyond the familiar.

The default path often revolves around mere existence, where individuals do things because they were told to, because it's what they read or heard. In stark contrast, a destined life is about truly living and embracing the audacity to step out of the confines that friends, parents, teachers, or society may attempt to box us into. Self-awareness plays a pivotal role, demanding that we not only recognize the individuality of each person's journey but also wholeheartedly accept it for ourselves. We often extol the virtues of the destined path when it pertains to others, but we may struggle to apply that same appreciation to our own lives. It is a journey of self-acceptance, understanding that our uniqueness is, in fact, our destiny, and embracing it without reservation.

# RECEIVE AND REFLECT - COURAGE

**My thoughts:**

In the face of obstacles, when others choose to step back, it becomes our cue to step forward, discerning the hidden opportunities within challenges. There's a tendency to overestimate what we could achieve if given the opportunities we lack, while simultaneously underestimating the transformative power of the opportunities already within our reach. It's a subtle yet profound realization that what we possess at this moment might be precisely what we need for the journey ahead. Embarking on this path requires courage, especially when confronted with confusion or obscured horizons. Personally, I encountered a shift in courage as my initial excuses gradually transformed into a hindrance fueled by unnecessary pettiness.

---

**Self-reflection questions:**

- What risk am I happy I took and why did it pay off?

- In which areas of my life can I be more courageous?

- What fears or challenges am I currently avoiding? Why?

---

# THE SUCCESSFUL ALSO CRY

Even the most accomplished individuals are not immune to the difficulties of life, but it is possible to persevere through these struggles and come out even stronger. "The Successful also cry" provides a deeper understanding of the human experience of success and empowers you to embrace your own vulnerabilities on your journey to boundless living.

# 9 THE SUCCESSFUL ALSO CRY

Many anticipated that 2020 would be the most exceptional year. People said that it would be the year of vision. The same way the year became an analogy for vision, the year also became the answer to a lot of people's prayers, yet they fell into victim hood because they lacked vision. As people around the world were anticipating the new year, partying their sorrows away and celebrating a new start, on the 31st of December 2019, the doctors told me that they found something suspicious in my body. My very own New Year revelation. I woke up in 2020 with more blurred vision than when I abruptly relocated to the United States.

Two months before the doctor's report, I found myself at the doctor's office on my birthday. I had taken the day off work and wanted to spend my birthday eating great food and watching funny movies. An unexpected ear clog resulted in me taking a trip to the doctor, because I was not going to let anything ruin my 21st birthday. The one thing I had always feared, but at the same time, never expected to actually happen to me, was going to see a doctor for one simple thing but coming out with news about something more tragic. I had seen it happen in Grey's Anatomy and Hollywood does such a great job in portraying such an occurrence that you will never think it could happen to you. Well, this was my reality.

On my 21st birthday, I walked into the doctor's office with a blocked ear and came out with the knowledge of an obscure lump, a tumor. My very own birthday consolation. For the next few months, I was walking in uncertainty. I did not know what it meant, but Google helped fill out a lot of the blanks, so much to the point that I thought I could diagnose myself!

As I wiped my eyes to see a new day, a new month, a new year, I held on to the things that I so easily took for granted. I expressed gratitude for my family, friends, and the support system. All of which I did not know how much I needed in months to come. In the second week of the new year, my biopsy results confirmed my greatest fear and hence forth, I embarked on the mission of gaining clarity in my situation and comfort in my sadness.

## Blurred Lines

Throughout the early stages of the new findings, I was interning at the same time. Physically and emotionally, I was in pain, and I did not know how to still be *professional*. I did not know if it was unprofessional of me to inform my manager about what was happening. I did not know if taking days or weeks off would make me look like a bad intern. The lines of being professionally acceptable and personally authentic became blurred many times, so much so that one day after signing into my laptop and checking emails at work, I went to the bathroom and broke down. The weight became too much., and I was tired of pretending like everything was okay, waiting until I came home before I stopped holding my breath. When I found the courage to finally take a breath, the Coronavirus disease (COVID-19) hit the United States. A pandemic that shook the world and shattered everyone's plans for the new year.

As the number of infected people increased around the world, my chances of getting surgery scheduled soon decreased. After weeks of contemplating whether to rely on a miracle or medicine to remove the tumor from my body, the choice became nonexistent as hospitals started rejecting non COVID-19 patients. The same way there was so much uncertainty about the state of the world, travel, education, etc. I had no idea when the next time I would be able to see my doctor was, not to talk about getting surgery. It was fair to say that my world, internally and externally, became a very uncertain place to reside, and slowly I became a resident of victimhood.

The first few months of 2020 were some of the loneliest

years I have felt. A unique form of loneliness – one that did not stem from the absence of people, but rather from their presence. People could not comprehend what I was going through so much to the extent that because I was known as this 'strong' person who had overcome many challenges, they assumed I would be fine and consequently withdrew into the background. I guess they thought it was flattering. Though from the outside, people thought I had it all together, on the inside, I was falling apart. Piece by piece. When people say that "it is lonely at the top", it is because sometimes they are waiting to be poured into, only to realize that they are staring down at a half empty cup.

This happened even when I moved to the United States. My friends thought that I had it all together and was now in this great land of opportunity, so they stopped checking up on me and too faded into the background. Again, flattering. If we look at our leaders and mentors -or even just someone who has more expertise than us in something- as having it all together, then we deprive ourselves of learning and deprive them of growing. When we look at mentorship relationships – you have the mentor and the mentee. If as a mentee, you behave in such a way that you only take from the mentor, not thinking that there is anything to give, you fall into the mindset that convinces you that your mentors' cup is already full. What people fail to acknowledge in this analogy, is that mentors have *many* cups, and not every one of them is full. While they may be pouring into you from the fullest cup, that doesn't mean the abundance you have to offer them will go to waste.

EVEN AN OVERFLOW IS A BLESSING.

When you rid yourself of this mentality and operate from a place of pouring into anyone and everyone, no matter their status or state, you subconsciously humble yourself and operate as a servant, and as you do so, you will be made great.

## Who encourages the encourager?

Entering 2020, my mind was brimming with ideas for diverse initiatives and dreams that I had long aspired to bring to life on LinkedIn and in the digital realm. However, as the weight of unforeseen challenges descended upon me,

I found myself reluctantly setting aside the personal brand I had carefully cultivated. I had mistakenly intertwined this digital persona with my identity, and as I gradually reduced my online presence, I felt like I was losing a part of myself that I had erroneously constructed around the idea of having a personal brand on LinkedIn. After three years of active digital engagement, the withdrawal symptoms were palpable, and I was compelled to confront and accept who I was without this virtual identity.

The need for validation and acceptance tugged at my core, yet I refused to hide behind a façade of perfection. Many of my friends marveled at my packed calendar, filled with speaking engagements with student organizations and constant calls with students. It was the life I had grown accustomed to, the life that provided validation and acceptance, and I wasn't ready to let it go. Little did I know that sometimes the most profound disruption can evolve into a remarkable blessing.

I often ponder whether I may have brought this sense of isolation upon myself. On LinkedIn, I had established a personal brand around my name, known as #BoundlessBlessing. Over the years, I had become the student who encouraged students, educated professionals, and empowered those in between. To my followers, I was seen as a LinkedIn Influencer; to my friends, I was perceived as someone who was always on the go. Neither role allowed me the space to simply breathe. Although the beginning of 2020 blurred my vision, it also afforded me the opportunity to exhale.

As time passed, my coping mechanisms underwent a transformation. Initially, I attempted to force activity, loading my plate with commitments, and striving to maintain the image of a 'busy' individual. Yet, what truly helped was surrendering to the person I thought I was and the path I believed I was meant to follow. It necessitated embracing the unknown and enduring the growing pains of self-discovery, which, as it turns out, were blessings in disguise.

In the ensuing months, I delved into my virtual spring term classes and embarked on my virtual internship with my dream company, Microsoft. While I was immensely grateful for these experiences, the burden I carried made it difficult to manage both academic and professional responsibilities. I couldn't confide in anyone within these spheres about my struggles, which only compounded the challenge. It was during this period that I made a firm decision: regardless of the grades I received or whether I secured a return offer, I would be gentle with myself. I knew what I had gone through and recognized the magnitude of emerging on the other side. It was also during this time that my doctor informed me that, given the rapid rise in COVID-19 cases, my anticipated surgery would likely be delayed by 2-3 months. I couldn't comprehend why all of this was happening, and in the current pandemic climate, the initially projected 2-3 months felt like an overly generous estimate.

During this period, I serendipitously stumbled upon a Mentorship Program organized by The Global Purpose Enterprise, an organization based in London, UK, driven by the vision of unlocking potential through Events & Mentorship for Young Black and Underrepresented

Visionaries. Amid the turbulence and chaos of the times, I yearned for something that could divert my mind from the negative and isolating thoughts that had been gnawing at me. Little did I anticipate that this Mentorship Program would emerge as a beacon of hope, a remedy for the solitude that had been weighing me down. As I progressively immersed myself in the program, both as a mentee and an ambassador, I experienced an incredible transformation in how I perceived and carried the burdens of my life. It wasn't about evading reality but about wholeheartedly embracing it and refusing to let it define me. I began to acquire the wisdom of finding contentment regardless of the circumstances that surrounded me.

SOMETIMES WE GET SO USED TO OUR CIRCUMSTANCES THAT WE SUCCUMB TO EXISTING, RATHER THAN LIVING.

In that phase of newfound contentment, I began to witness a profound shift in my life's trajectory. Come July, I was finally able to meet with my doctor after an agonizing five-month wait, and to my immense relief, we booked my surgery for August. This was a pivotal moment, not solely because of the upcoming surgery but because during that very appointment, my doctor delivered astonishing news: one of my tumors had vanished. It was an astounding revelation that left me in a state of utter disbelief. I had encountered a miracle while eagerly awaiting medical intervention to bring about my recovery. As the date for my surgery drew nearer, I had undergone a profound shift in my perspective on the situation. I realized that the delay in securing the surgery didn't obstruct my healing; instead, it marked an essential purification process I needed to endure to emerge as refined gold.

By the close of that summer, I had achieved a stellar record, securing a majority of A's in my classes and landing a full-time position with Microsoft following my graduation. During the post-surgery period, as I recovered and reflected on the arduous journey I'd traversed, I couldn't help but contemplate the full scope of my experiences. While #BoundlessBlessing could post on LinkedIn about my triumphant academic performance and internship with Microsoft that summer, no one could truly fathom the tribulations I had surmounted. In that moment, I had gained a profound understanding of the adage that not everything that glitters is gold; rather, gold is the product of enduring pressure and refining.

## Inwards and Onwards

In August, I had my surgery. I was so relieved, especially after all that waiting. I remember my doctor saying that the tumor was more aggressive than she thought, so taking it out became more difficult and recovering from the surgery took much longer than anticipated. I was so excited to embark on my senior year on a clean slate free of pain, anxiety, and uncertainty. And I did, until January 2021. At the beginning of 2021, I found out that my tumor had returned. What I had to learn is that following Christ does not make me exempt from struggle. I somehow thought that all problems would disappear once I'm no longer in the year 2020. The year of the global pandemic. The year that everything shut down. The year that changed everything. What hit me the most is that I felt like history was repeating itself. Here I was, almost in the 6th month of 2021, waiting for another breakthrough that will allow me to have another surgery before my graduation. More realistically, before I start working. The longer I waited, the more I asked myself "Where is God?" "Why would God let me go through this again?" and the more I've understood that the presence of my pain didn't mean the absence of my God.

By sharing my journey in this book, I hope to encourage the people who have no choice but to live with a condition, illness, or pain. I applaud them for the number of doctor and hospital visits they have had to endure, the times they've cried out "why does it have to be a part of me?!" and the days they've counted down for a miracle, yet still choose to be here, to fight, to keep walking, despite the uncertainty, despite the inevitable. If this is you, you are not alone. I am so proud of you, and I hope that you have people to believe things for you when you don't have the strength to believe any more. Until you do. May the tears you have sown, reap a harvest of joy.

## YOU CAN'T HEAL A WOUND YOU DON'T KNOW YOU HAVE.

The year 2021 got me thinking about what it's like to remove something that was never good for you in the first place.

The removal of a tumor the size of a strawberry meant that I would have to learn to be comfortable with seeing the unattractive indent in my skin of where the lump once was. I had to make a tradeoff. It's the reality of having to get rid of something that harms more than it heals. You might be reading this and not have a chronic illness, disease, or pain to monitor or manage, but what are you allowing to grow and take over your life? I hope you take the opportunity to examine your life for open wounds, poisonous weeds, and malignant influences, while you still have the chance to heal them, cut them loose and remove them. Sometimes you might feel lost in the wilderness. Sometimes you will feel overwhelmed by the world. Sometimes you will feel alone. I need you to know that despite what things may look like, you are truly blessed, and you will get through this.

# RECEIVE AND REFLECT - INTERNAL DEVELOPMENT

**My thoughts:**

Knowledge entails grasping patterns from the information we acquire, while wisdom involves comprehending underlying principles. Internal growth occurs when we reflect on and analyze our past patterns and behaviors, urging us to examine the intricate tapestry woven by these elements in our lives. This introspective process unveils valuable insights, fostering the development of emotional intelligence and self-awareness. By discerning these patterns, we equip ourselves with the tools to deepen our understanding of both our individual selves and our role in the broader world.

**Self-reflection questions:**

- Am I able to extract valuable lessons from my mistakes and negative experiences?

- How do I navigate and express vulnerability with those close to me when facing challenges?

- What habits or coping mechanisms have proven effective in managing stress and adversity, and which ones may need reassessment?

# BOUND TO BE BOUNDLESS

Content Warning: This story contains sensitive and potentially distressing themes related to depression, self-harm, and mental health. Reader discretion is advised, and please take care of your well-being while reading. If you or someone you know is struggling with these issues, don't hesitate to seek help or reach out to a mental health professional. You are not alone, and there is support available.

# 10 BOUND TO BE BOUNDLESS

Difficult situations never leave us the way they found us. I sat on a bench, next to Philadelphia's Schuylkill River in the midnight hour, thinking of how I found myself there. Not physically, but mentally. How difficult must my situation have gotten that I did not care how and where someone would find me in the morning? I did not want to be found. I wanted to finally disappear into the depths of the water, and let my shackles sink to the seabed. Looking up at the high-rise buildings that swept through the city of

Philadelphia, I could see how small I was. Though the light from the buildings lit up the sky, impenetrable darkness was all around me. The hour was interrupted by hints of bike riders taking in the midnight breeze, couples on their night walk and homeless people finding shelter. Even in the darkest hour, life went on around me. My body felt chained to the bench as I endured a battle in my mind, that I was one fence away from losing. I was tired of running from my past and fighting it with the little strength I had after running. So, I sat. I waited. I cried. I mourned the woman I had not given myself a chance to grow into. Creeping into my head were the words from Elevation Worship's 'Here in the Presence':

"I know your past is broken. You can move on. It is over now. Here in the presence of the Lord. Tired of running, running. Be still and know He's in control."

I had become so numb to my surroundings that I forgot I was listening to music. The lyrics pierced my heart and spoke to me. The simple melody was slowly releasing me of the chains of fear and anxiety. Without a care of who could hear me or who was listening, I started singing the words out: "Here I lay my burdens down. Lose my worries in your love. Casting every care on you. I have carried them enough." I meant every word. These words were the seeds for change, transformation, and hope. I saw the power of praise break barriers, restore energy, and connect me to the source of every good thing. I used to think that the dark, grey cloud and shadow that was cast over me was my protection, but I did not realize that the cloud was preventing me from walking in light.

That night, I stretched out my hands to receive God's mercy and surrendered myself to His will.

MY PAIN WAS PART OF THE PROCESS THAT WOULD PRODUCE MY PURPOSE AND PERFECT HIS PROMISE.

That night I let go of my identity that was bound to the heartache and deep darkness of my past and took up another identity, a boundless one. An identity rooted in Jesus Christ. I was finally grounded and settled. In the midst of my insecurity, I found my security in Christ. It was through His grace that I was saved that night.

In the realm of human experience, there's a shadow that can stealthily affect our emotions. This shadow is called depression. It's the feeling of numbness that can smother our emotions and make life seem challenging. It can make our days blur together, and we might feel like we're just going through the motions. In the past, I had dealt with depression. Some days, I had moments of clarity and hope, but most of the time, depression had a strong hold on me. It's not just something I experienced alone; it also affected my relationships. In a world where most of our interactions are through screens and phone calls, things get even more complicated.

Depression, self-harm, and even thoughts of self-harm can be difficult to understand. They are often hidden behind a facade of normalcy during calls or messages. It's easy for someone to miss the signs. The gap between what's inside and what's projected outward is a reminder of how complex the human mind can be.

In this confusing situation, there's a silent plea for guidance and support. It's an acknowledgment that, despite feeling helpless, we hope for healing, mending the broken pieces, and bringing light to the darkest corners of the mind. This is the quiet prayer that we hold onto. This is a topic often kept hidden, rarely discussed in the church or within families. It's important to break the silence and have open conversations to remove the stigma and taboo around mental health. Not just for the sake of our relationships but for the future, for our children, and for our families.

I watched a TV show where a character engaged in self-harm, and it reminded me of my own struggle. I carry the scars of self-inflicted pain, etched on my wrists, as a constant battle against the numbness within.

As I dealt with this internal turmoil, I tried various ways to numb the pain – pills, alcohol, and self-inflicted wounds. These self-inflicted wounds were my way of trying to feel something, anything, in the face of depression.

But I wondered, when did the emotional pain in my soul

turn into physical self-harm? This journey through the complexities of the human mind is both haunting and hopeful, a testament to resilience and the unwavering spirit that seeks a path to healing, no matter how obscure it may seem.

## Free Indeed

Have you ever experienced such a dark place? Where did your light come from? I thought that it would be impossible to see the light after that dark night. Months leading up to this encounter, Courtney, one of the Campus Ministers prophesied the following words:

"You're going to be able to lead people that have struggled with some of the things you have and set them free."

It was difficult to believe. I saw myself as a leader, that was not the problem. The problem was knowing that I would have to go through so much more, for the sake of helping set others free. It is not until you have been held captive, that you can fully appreciate freedom. The bible talks about Paul and Silas, who were imprisoned, beaten yet still praised God. What caught my attention in their story was how, when they were praying and praising, it was not only them that became free. "At once all the prison doors flew open, and everyone's chains came loose." (Acts 16:26). It is through the words of my testimony that I hope you will set yourself free from whatever you are held captive by.

## Restricted to Be Without Restriction

Physical change was always a constant growing up. I did not grow up in the safety of being stationary. Rather, I found myself being stationed in obscure settings. It was a major theme in my life that affected my identity, relationships, mindset, and religious outlook. I allowed my past to define me, leading me to carry the burden of every bad thing that ever happened to me. I experienced falling in with the wrong crowd, but also being afraid to commit to friendships because of the fear of moving. I was in constant battle with my state of mind which caused me to build walls and become a victim of my world. I blamed God for giving me an abnormal life and thought I was being punished for something I did not know I did. Yet, He gave me courage to face the hardship of my past, the shame, guilt, bitterness,

BOUND TO BE BOUNDLESS

lies, anger and rejection. Though I felt deprived of physical, emotional, and mental freedom, I have come to trust and believe that there is a reason for everything. Maybe I was surrounded by borders, so that I could appreciate what was beyond the walls. Maybe, I was chained, for the purpose of being set free.

## Destined to Be Without Limits

When I look back at my story of depression, questioning identity, feeling misunderstood and transitioning from one place to another, I cannot help but think about a verse in the bible that talks about perseverance. James 1:12 says:

> BLESSED IS THE ONE WHO PERSEVERES UNDER TRIAL BECAUSE, HAVING STOOD THE TEST, THAT PERSON WILL RECEIVE THE CROWN OF LIFE THAT THE LORD HAS PROMISED TO THOSE WHO LOVE HIM.

It is an encouragement for those who face trials and tribulations in their lives. A symbol of recognition and honor upon anyone who faithfully serves Him. Destined to be without limits means that the safety and security I have found in Christ, has given me strength to stand up against tribulations. It means that He has delivered me from bondage and has replaced the darkness in my heart, with his limitless love and grace. Even when I do not understand the process, I must trust His promise. Even when everything in my life changes, I continue on because I know God has promised to never abandon me, rather love, comfort, and protect me. It is in His nature for me to live a free and boundless life.

## Internal Development, External Realities

All my life, I have moved. Schools, countries, continents. I anticipated change so much to the point that I started living with a temporary mindset. I lacked vision for my life. Though from the outside, people thought I had it all together, on the inside, I was falling apart, but also falling into place. Through my highs and lows,

I HAVE BEEN REDEFINED BY THE WORLD ON THE OUTSIDE AND REFINED BY HIS WORD ON THE INSIDE.

My circumstance and broken background did not need to define me the way I let it, instead I had to create a new definition for it. Internal Development is the growth that happens when someone uses their own resources to grow. It is the process of turning your walls into bridges, tests into testimonies and conflict into confidence. My faith has become what is my foundation and motivation. It is what keeps me going when I want to quit, it is what convicts me when I become stagnant, and it is what gets me out of bed in the morning when I take life for granted. It is the internal development that allows me to persevere, during external conflicts.

Whoever you are, wherever you come from, and whatever you have been through, while you are being crushed, pruned, purified, cleaned, molded, and transformed, know that God can use every season, every situation, and every setback for your good and His glory.

From bound, to boundless.

# FOR SUCH A TIME AS THIS

"For Such a Time as This" delves into the concept of divine timing and how our experiences, both good and bad, can be used to prepare us for the purpose and calling that God has for us. Explore how Esther's story in the Bible serves as a reminder that we have been placed in our current circumstances "for such a time as this" and that we should trust in God's plan even when it may seem difficult or uncertain.

# 11 FOR SUCH A TIME AS THIS

SOMETIMES IT IS THE PROCESS, NOT THE
OUTCOME, THAT IS THE MOST REWARDING.

I've found that many people think that if everything looks
somewhat perfect from the outside, then it must be true
within. Better yet, I have seen that though the process is
rough, people would prefer to appreciate the rough process
of someone else's journey, rather than appreciate their own.
There has become a disconnect between what people
assume to be true and know to be true. All that glitters is
not gold. It was the purification process of my life, that

piqued the interest of strangers, friends and even family. It was the struggles, hiccups, and atypical journey that people resonated with. Through my life, you see me as someone who was bound to my identity, negative voices, bad friends, past circumstances, but came out boundless. It was the only way. My hope for you, dear reader, in reading about my story is you too will be able to apply your wealth of knowledge, reflections, and lessons learned in your life.

As the world became my stomping ground, and each country became a classroom, I found myself being assigned and tested, over and over and over again. Living in 4 different countries on 3 different continents of the world opened my horizons. It has made me appreciate the values of humanity, although understood and lived differently. My experience as a global citizen opened me up to living differently in the sense that I had to learn how to make the most of where I was. I didn't know how 'quickly' I would have to relocate, and waiting to find out, could have cost me many experiences. These experiences helped me understand life in a new way because going through life, seeing myself as a victim of my circumstance, caused me to live life as a prisoner in my own mind. It was through my own personal experiences that supported this understanding. The fact that I have come to identify myself with all the different cultural contexts, helps me to recognize unity but also diversity. I learned the importance of defining my own identity, but also not to attach myself to my identity. It was a surprising revelation to hold onto. One of my key takeaways from this 'non-attachment of identity' process was that defining something and letting something define you is completely different. If I continued to allow my identity to define me, and therefore attach myself to it - many doors would have closed that I didn't know were open in the first place. I may have been forced to learn from my experiences, but it was ultimately down to me. Now, I get to choose.

This book is about identifying the challenges of life and going forward anyway. Being bound but choosing to be boundless. It is about connecting with inner conviction to question family, friends, and situations toward striving for better systems and living a fulfilling life. Through my experiences of being surrounded by people, yet still feeling lonely, misunderstood, and scared, I learned the value and voice of people, including my own. I learned that as much as people can lift you up, they can also bring you down. At the end of the day, how you value your voice and how you speak to yourself, trumps it all. I had to evaluate the level of permission I have given those around me - learning that, If I give power to the people, it should not be to my own detriment. I was encouraged to face my fears head on and be the change that someone else would need. If I lacked conviction, I may not be where I am now. I would have gotten lost in the process and drowned in the shallow waters of life. I saw how standing up for myself wasn't just for me, but for those who will come after me.

Writing this book felt like a therapy session and extended journal entry, all in one. Writing this book was tough because I knew I had to not only recall past experiences but travel back to those times in my life. I had to presently feel what I was not able to fully feel in the past. There was a lot I could not see back then that I see now. It was during this reflection time that allowed me to cry, feel anger, laugh, appreciate the old and anticipate the new.

When I dug up my own stories, I found enlightening evidence about the roots of my problems and why I had to go through certain experiences. Stories about my experiences with friends allowed me to see why it was difficult to steward friendships. Stories about my reactions to relocation allowed me to understand where my strength and adaptability came from. I gathered aligning facts about the imperfection of social media, supporting the fact that all that glitters is not gold. Being able to analyze the impact of third culture individuals like me, not only gave me peace knowing that I wasn't alone, but also empowered me to continue sharing my story in hopes that it can help another third culture individual. I came to realize how everything I've been through landed me where I am now.

Looking back at my past has left me feeling more grateful than anything. I think that sometimes when we look back, with no understanding of why certain things happened, it fills us with anxiety and fear. To be where I am now is a great accomplishment for me. To be able to understand why certain things happened feels liberating to say the least.

I am now at a place in my life, where I feel and believe that I have processed the difficult seasons in my life, in order to create a fulfilling future. Viewing my life now through a reflective lens, encourages me to process conflicts and concerns in real time, rather than years down the line. Not only am I able to do it, but I'm able to see the importance in doing it. As a leader, and through my personal experiences, I have developed empathy in a way that I can relate to people in different walks of life. I have become a more intentional friend, who is no longer afraid of commitment or transparency. As a global citizen, I do not allow my background to confine me, rather liberate me.

As I bring "Bound to be Boundless" to a close, I want to express my deep gratitude to you, the reader. Your journey alongside me in these pages is an honor. I hope you've found the courage to reevaluate your own life, challenge your assumptions, and, most importantly, embrace the boundless potential within you. That you come to believe, that you were created for such a time as this. That your story is still unfolding. Thank you for being a part of mine.

# RECEIVE AND REFLECT

Here is a compilation of all of the "receive and reflect" thoughts and questions that were dotted through the book.

# RECEIVE AND REFLECT - COMPARISON

**My thoughts:**

Comparison isn't just about what someone else possesses; it's often about how they navigate and achieve things with what they've got. It's a disservice to yourself to stack your journey and story against someone else's. The key is to stay focused on your purpose, and when you're truly engaged in your own path, comparison loses its power to distract.

Simply put, if we mind our own business and run with the grace tailor-made for our journey, we emerge victorious every time. Success isn't about coveting someone else's grass; it's about tending to our own and watching it flourish. By embracing our unique narrative, acknowledging the journey behind us, and eagerly anticipating what lies ahead, we not only appreciate our own story but also rise to the levels of those we admire.

---

**Self-reflection questions:**

- How do I balance the different parts of my multicultural identity?

- Think about a time when you had to adjust to a new culture. How did I handle the change, and what helped me adapt?

---

# RECEIVE AND REFLECT - PERSEVERANCE

**My thoughts:**

Navigating and implementing change is no small feat for those carrying the weight of the task. Perseverance, a quality born out of overcoming adversity, isn't cultivated in the midst of a trouble-free life. There was a time when I believed that perseverance could only be developed in the midst of a comfortable and smooth sailing life. However, I've come to understand that this trait emerges from experiences of stumbling and picking oneself up again. It's about the resilience found in standing tall after a fall, and the cumulative strength gained with each setback that equips individuals to thrive in the face of challenges. Amid various trials, one that stands out vividly is the period when I juggled classes and internships for three consecutive summers. Each summer brought its own waves of hopelessness and imposter syndrome, yet the experience from the previous summer served as a wellspring of strength for the next.

**Self-reflection questions:**

- What hurdles am I determined to conquer? Why?

- In reaching this point, what obstacles have I already triumphed over?

- Do specific habits or routines help me sustain perseverance?

# RECEIVE AND REFLECT - FAITH

**My thoughts:**
Growing up, I used to always hear the testimonies and stories of those who grew up in church their entire life or grew up in a Christian home. Through my eyes, they were the "model" Christian's, the perfect ones. It wasn't until a few years after I was saved, that I had to realize that no one is perfect, even a Christian. Especially a Christian. Each Christian is travelling their own, personal journey with God and in their faith. It will look different for everyone, and in different seasons but it's important to hold onto the fact that there is grace for a given race. Meaning, one doesn't need to look to the right or left of them, there is no competing with Christianity. Parents can't force it. Knowing God and accepting Him, is a promise that happens between you and Him only.

---

**Self-reflection questions:**
- How has my perception of faith transformed throughout my life's journey?

- What significance does my personal journey with God hold for me, and which aspects of it carry the most importance in my life?

- What do I perceive as my life's purpose and mission?

---

# RECEIVE AND REFLECT - IDENTITY

## My thoughts:

Start from scratch, as if the slate is blank. Often, it's cluttered with the echoes of others' words and the imprints of our observations. In the pursuit of crafting an image, our true identity can fade into the background. While image is what we project, identity is the essence of who we truly are. Amid the effort to escape aspects of ourselves we dislike, our identity can be easily forgotten. Allocate time to delve into both your internal and external self—acknowledging both the commendable and the challenging. It's often the facets we may not admire that empower us to make a meaningful impact in the world. Embrace the entirety of your identity, for it is the authentic foundation from which your unique contributions can blossom.

---

**Self-reflection questions:**

- Do my projected image and authentic identity align consistently?

- In what manner has my past contributed to shaping my identity, and in what ways do I aspire to evolve or transform?

---

# RECEIVE AND REFLECT - LEADERSHIP

**My thoughts:**
The common misbelief surrounding leadership is that it solely accompanies seniority or a paid position. I've reshaped my understanding of leadership—it's not confined to titles but encompasses actions and behaviors that inspire people toward a shared goal or greater good. Don't delay taking on a leadership role until it's officially bestowed upon you or tied to a job title. Leadership isn't exclusive to the workplace; it can manifest in any situation. Regardless of your current circumstances, you have the capacity to lead by seizing the initiative. Often, the most transformative leaders are those who recognize that leadership isn't about authority; it's about influence and the ability to spark positive change. So, don't underestimate the power you hold to lead in your daily interactions, be it within a team project, a community initiative, or even a casual conversation.

---

**Self-reflection questions:**
- In my view, what does success truly mean?

- What qualities of an effective leader do I currently possess?

- Can I find chances to mentor or guide others, even if I don't hold a conventional leadership position?

---

## RECEIVE AND REFLECT- RESOURCEFULNESS

**My thoughts:**

It is no surprise that life comes with its fair share of financial, academic, spiritual, physical, emotional, and mental challenges. These challenges force us into thinking that we do not have what we need to overcome those challenges. What we find is that the problem is not related to the lack of resources, but the inability to be resourceful. By challenging assumptions and questioning things, we open ourselves to see our problems from a renewed perspective. We start to see things from a place of advantage rather than disadvantage. An opportunity rather than an obstacle. Sometimes we have to create the solution that we want to see.

---

**Self-reflection questions:**

- Who has encountered a similar challenge, and what strategies did they employ to overcome it?

- If a solution isn't readily available, can I, or someone within my network, generate a viable solution?

- What resources am I lacking and how can I use what I have to bridge the gap?

---

# RECEIVE AND REFLECT - RELATIONSHIPS

**My thoughts:**

As I've gone through life, I've seen how having or not having relationships can mess with how I see and value people. There was this phase when I thought I could do without friendships or relationships, like it was me against the world. The idea of getting close to someone freaked me out – the thought that I could get ditched, let down, or just shoved aside. But as the years rolled on, I figured out how crucial relationships are for my own growth. Some folks think being picky about who you hang with and being intentional about relationships are the same thing. But I've learned it's not just about being picky; it's about being careful with who you let into your life and putting effort into the relationships you decide to keep. Those connections really shape who you are. We're not built to go through this life all alone. No matter how many times you've been let down or left behind, there are people out there who'll lift you up and make sure you know you're seen and loved.

**Self-reflection questions:**
- What are my love languages (to give and receive)?

- Which negative trait do I aim to release from my life?

- Who have I given excessive influence and access to in my life?

# RECEIVE AND REFLECT - COURAGE

**My thoughts:**

In the face of obstacles, when others choose to step back, it becomes our cue to step forward, discerning the hidden opportunities within challenges. There's a tendency to overestimate what we could achieve if given the opportunities we lack, while simultaneously underestimating the transformative power of the opportunities already within our reach. It's a subtle yet profound realization that what we possess at this moment might be precisely what we need for the journey ahead. Embarking on this path requires courage, especially when confronted with confusion or obscured horizons. Personally, I encountered a shift in courage as my initial excuses gradually transformed into a hindrance fueled by unnecessary pettiness.

---

**Self-reflection questions:**

- What risk am I happy I took and why did it pay off?

- In which areas of my life can I be more courageous?

- What fears or challenges am I currently avoiding? Why?

---

# RECEIVE AND REFLECT - INTERNAL
## DEVELOPMENT

**My thoughts:**
Knowledge entails grasping patterns from the information we acquire, while wisdom involves comprehending underlying principles. Internal growth occurs when we reflect on and analyze our past patterns and behaviors, urging us to examine the intricate tapestry woven by these elements in our lives. This introspective process unveils valuable insights, fostering the development of emotional intelligence and self-awareness. By discerning these patterns, we equip ourselves with the tools to deepen our understanding of both our individual selves and our role in the broader world.

---

**Self-reflection questions:**
- Am I able to extract valuable lessons from my mistakes and negative experiences?

- How do I navigate and express vulnerability with those close to me when facing challenges?

- What habits or coping mechanisms have proven effective in managing stress and adversity, and which ones may need reassessment?

---

# ABOUT THE AUTHOR

Blessing Adogame is an accomplished global citizen dedicated to empowering individuals from all walks of life. Born and raised in four distinct countries – Nigeria, Germany, Scotland, and the United States – she has had the unique opportunity to absorb the richness of diverse cultures, which has profoundly shaped her perspective on the world. From an early age, Blessing's nomadic upbringing instilled in her a deep appreciation for learning, adaptability, and personal growth. Every transition to a new country presented her with fresh challenges and valuable lessons. Rather than being deterred by obstacles, she embraced them as opportunities for self-discovery and development.

# Notes

---

[i] Messinger, H. Dis-like: How Social Media Feeds into Perfectionism, 19 Nov. 2019.

[ii] Oswal, N. M. An Immigrant in America: The Idea of Home, 30 Sept. 2017.

[iii] Oswal, N. M. An Immigrant in America: The Idea of Home, 30 Sept. 2017.

Printed in Great Britain
by Amazon

32822486R00108